Success. guides

Standard Grade
Physical Education

✕ Malcolm Thorburn ✕

Contents

The body – training and its effects

Skills and techniques – techniques

Skills and techniques – ways of developing skill

Skills and techniques – mechanical principles

Examinations

Nature and purpose

Individual or team activities

- An individual activity is where you perform on your own.
- A team activity is where you perform with others.
- An example of an individual activity would be singles tennis. However, tennis could be a team activity if you are performing as part of a doubles team. Some team games have many more players; rugby union has 15 players, for example.

Top-Tip
Some activities are mostly performed individually (e.g. squash) or as part of a team (e.g. volleyball). Other activities can be performed both on your own and as part of a team (e.g. tennis).

Directly competitive, indirectly competitive or non-competitive activies

- Some activities are competitive and some are non-competitive.
- Competitive activities are either directly or indirectly competitive.
- In an individual directly competitive activity (badminton) you have a direct influence on your opponent's performance. Likewise, in a directly competitive team activity (football) you can tackle your opponent.
- In an indirectly competitive activity (trampoline) you do not have direct contact with opponents. Non-competitive activities (hill-walking) are activities where you participate for your own pleasure rather than directly or indirectly against other performers or teams.

Top-Tip
Different individual and team activities can be directly competitive, indirectly competitive or non-competitive.

Directly competitive – team activity (football) 	Indirectly competitive activity (trampoline) 
Directly competitive – individual activity (badminton – singles) 	Non competitive (hill-walking) 

Objective scoring methods

- The outcome of different team and individual activities are decided by a variety of objective or subjective scoring methods.
- Winning by objective scoring methods includes: most goals (football); runs (cricket) and points (rugby).
- Some activities feature a range of different objective scoring systems. For example, within athletics the time taken is used in various running races (100m, 200m, 400m, 800m) and height and distance measurement are used to decide different jumping and throwing events. Objective scoring is measured by definite means – time, points, etc.

Athletics objective scoring – Time	Athletics objective scoring – Height	Athletics objective scoring – Distance

Subjective scoring methods

- Subjective scoring methods are based on the opinions and values of those judging performances.
- In making scoring decisions judges need to consider many different factors. For example, in rhythmic gymnastics the range and quality of different movements and use of space and projection is considered.
- A few activities combine objective and subjective scoring methods. In ski-jumping, the final mark is based on the distance jumped (objective) and the quality of the jump (subjective).

Top-Tip

The outcome of different team and individual activities, which are either directly competitive or indirectly competitive, is decided by a variety of objective or subjective scoring methods.

Reasons for participating in different activities

There are many reasons why you might be more interested in some activities than others. It could be that the physical challenge of activities appeals to you; it could be through the different social benefits that participation offers through meeting other people; it could also be that the health benefits of regular active participation are appealing to you.

Actions required in different activities

A further reason which might influence your preferences for different activities could be the actions required when actively participating. Compare and contrast the different types of actions in a range of different activities.

Jumping	Kicking	Throwing
Striking	Rotating	Stretching

Quick Test

1. What type of activity is volleyball?

2. What type of activity is table tennis?

3. Name one outdoor pursuit which is non-competitive.

4. What type of activity is archery?

5. What type of activity is netball?

6. Copy and complete the following grid.

Activity	Objective / Subjective	How results are decided
Basketball		
Rugby union		
Gymnastics		
Badminton		

Answers 1. A team activity which is directly competitive. 2. An individual and or team activity which is directly competitive. 3. Hill-walking. 4. An individual activity which is indirectly competitive. 5. A team activity which is directly competitive. 6. Basketball / Objective / The team which scores the highest number of points wins. Rugby union / Objective / The team which scores the highest number of points wins. Points can be scored by a try (5 points), try conversion kick (2 points) or by a penalty kick or drop goal (3 points). Gymnastics / Subjective / Marks awarded by judgement of the quality of gymnastics movements. Badminton/ Subjective / Number of games won. Each game is up to 15 points.

Creativity

What is creativity?

- Creativity is about the unusual, the unexpected and the unique. Creativity occurs in most activities where you devise and create solutions to different problems. Being creative is important for all levels of performer.

- In many team and individual activities you are **re-creative** as a performer. Many of the moves or manoeuvres have been used before; however, you are using them in your own unique way.

Creativity in different activities

- In directly competitive team games using imagination and creative flair can create attacking advantages and create uncertainty in those who are trying to mark you.

- In indirectly competitive gymnastics floor events you use imagination and creative flair to ensure that space is used effectively by covering all parts of the floor space available.

Top-Tip
Remember there are many different ways of being creative in activities.

Gymnastics floor sequence example

Name:	Class:
Date:	
Length of routine (time)	Music used (if any)

Skills:
Flight
Star jump ✓✓
Tuck jump ✓
Straddle / pike ✓

Rotation
Forward roll ✓✓
Backward roll ✓
Dive forward roll ✓

Inversion
Handstand ✓
Cartwheel
Round off

Balance
Headstand ✓
Shoulder stand ✓✓
Arabesque ✓✓

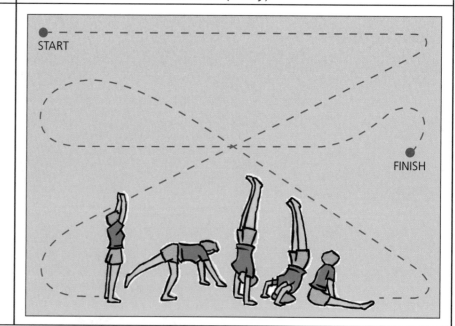

Creative qualities desirable: Changes in body shape ✓✓✓,
Changes in direction ✓✓, Sudden explosive movements ✓,
Light sustained movements ✓✓✓, Movements finishing in a balance ✓✓✓

Analysis of gymnastic floor sequence: Varied skills and creative qualities included. Further refinement should consider adding more inversions and sudden explosive movements to sequence.

Creativity as expression

- In some activities being creative plays an important part in expressing ideas and emotions in new and original ways. Often performance is linked to accompanying music.
- Good expressive ideas enable your performance to be interpreted easily and allow you to show different emotions and moods in your presentation.

Dance example

Contrast the two pictures of the different dancers.
What emotion and mood do you think they are trying to project?
You will probably consider that while the picture of the four dancers projects control and strength, the picture of the two dancers instead expresses sensitivity.

Top-Tip
In games disguising your intentions is a useful way to show creativity.

Basketball example

Sometimes when shooting in basketball, attacking players will fake to take a jump shot. If the defender takes the fake and jumps upwards this provides the attacking player with time and space to drive towards the basket and take a lay-up shot.

Quick Test

1. Explain two ways creativity could improve your presentation in a gymnastics floor sequence.
2. Give one example of how you could disguise your intentions in badminton.

Answers 1. Vary the skills and creative qualities included in the sequence. 2. You could set-up as if you were going to play an overhead clear shot. Then you could slow the racquet speed down and play an overhead drop shot to the front of your opponent's court instead.

Principles of play

Fundamental principles of play

Applying the fundamental principles of play in team games enables you to create attacking opportunities (for example, through creating an overload) and consider how to control space in defence (for example, through applying pressure on opponents).

- The fundamental principles of play in many team games involve **width and depth** in attack and defence; and **delay** in defence.
- Evaluating your team **roles and responsibilities** and individual **strengths and weaknesses** will be important in selecting tactics and planning performances which effectively apply principles of play.

Volleyball example

There are six positions / **roles** in volleyball; these are labelled in diagrams to make them easier to remember (see Volleyball 1 picture). A rally in volleyball begins with a service (see Volleyball 2 picture). The player after serving moves to his position inside the court after hitting the service.

On the receiving side, the setter is standing by the net in the middle, and waiting for the ball to be played to her. The remainder of the team's **responsibility** is to get their arms under the service, and pass (dig) the ball to the setter. The receivers are in a W-formation in order to cover the **width and depth** of the court in the most effective way possible. Each player has to check their own position and that of their team mates at this stage.

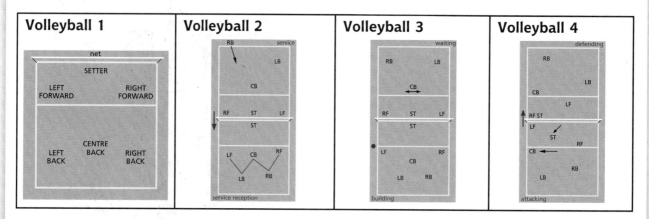

Next (see Volleyball 3 picture) the setter will volley (set) the ball to one of the forwards. The two forwards are standing behind the 3-metre line preparing for the set. The defending team positions their net players close to the net facing the opponents' court. Next (see Volleyball 4 picture) the left forward has moved up to the net and is jumping in an attempt to hit (spike) the ball towards the other team's court with one hand. The defending forwards try to block the spike while the rear court back players try to cover the court (width and depth) as best they can.

Principles of play examples

In team games effective communication will help your team to make the most of your strengths and limit your weaknesses. For example, in volleyball, clearly calling that you will play the next shot helps your team mates prepare to move and react.

Delay in defence

When defending it is often better to slow down attacking players by 'backing away' from them. This delays attacking players from getting past you and enables other defenders a little more time to organise the defence. Delay in defence works best in certain areas of the playing area. Generally, as attackers get closer to the scoring target delay in defence becomes less possible to use as a principle of play.

> **Top-Tip**
> When explaining principles of play try to apply explanations of strengths and weaknesses to the principles of width, depth and delay

Hockey example

In this example, the defender is a few metres away from the attacking player and has delayed tackling so far. The defender is trying to force the attacking player into the central area of the pitch where there is a greater chance that other team mates can help tackle the attacking player.

Quick Test

1. What is meant by width in attack in a team game?

2. What is meant by depth in attack in a team game?

3. What is meant by width in defence in a team game?

4. What is meant by depth in defence in a team game?

5. What is meant by delay in defence in a team game?

Answers 1. Ensuring that players use the full width of the playing area to help create effective attacks. 2. Ensuring that attacking players are supported by team mates. This helps retain possession, for example, by enabling the furthest forward attacker to pass backwards to his / her midfield players. 3. Ensuring that players cover the full width of the playing area to help limit effective attacks. 4. Ensuring that defending players are supported by team mates. This helps secure possession; for example, if one defender is passed by an attacker, the next defender may be able to secure possession. 5. Slowing down attacking players by 'backing away' from them. This delays attacking players from getting past you.

Tactics 1

What is a tactic?

- A tactic is a specific way of carrying out a particular strategy and of applying in action principles of play common in games.
- The choice of tactic will often depend upon the time left and the score within a game.
- The overall aim of a tactic is to play to your individual and team / group strengths, and to attempt to exploit your opponent's weaknesses.

Applying tactics

In all types of activities your planning is designed to highlight how your strengths and weaknesses can help performance. At times, you also should consider the strengths and weaknesses of opponents. Tactics often need to be changed if your opponents change their tactics, if you are losing near the end of a game and need to score and, by contrast, if you are winning near the end of a game and need to protect your lead.

Tennis example

Counter-attacking is one tennis tactic which can be effective. The overall idea is to wait for the right attacking opportunity. Opposing players can often make mistakes when they try to take the initiative in the rally. Pictures one to four show the type of rally which can take place. Player A is slowing down the speed of the rally by making his opponent (Player B) move to the wide areas of the court to play a return shot. Once the opponent becomes used to a slow rally, a faster shot is often enough to win him the point – in this example through a stronger more forceful shot down the line (Picture 5).

Top-Tip

The overall aim of a tactic is to play to your individual / team strengths, and to attempt to exploit your opponent's weaknesses

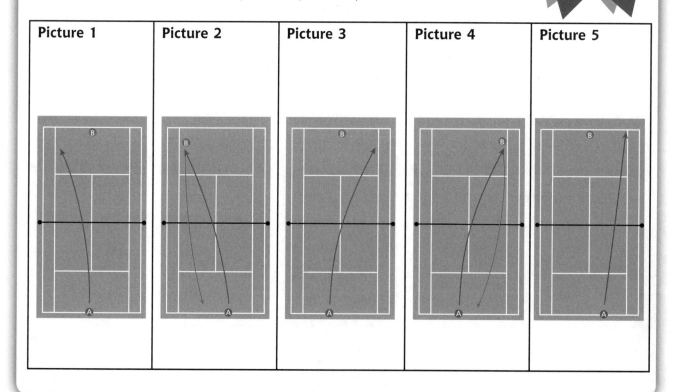

Picture 1	Picture 2	Picture 3	Picture 4	Picture 5

Physical and personal qualities

- For your tactics to be effective it is important that you and other team mates have good physical and personal qualities.
- Physical qualities include different aspects of fitness (cardiorespiratory, muscular endurance, speed, strength, power, flexibility).
- Personal qualities such as determination, courage and self-confidence are also important.

Qualities		

Physical qualities	Has good strength for driving to the basket and completing lay up shot.	Has good flexibility to show extension in jump on beam.
Personal qualities	Is determined to get close to the basket before shooting.	Is confident and courageous enough to perform difficult skills in front of an audience.

Effective communication in tactics

- For your tactics to be effective it is important that you and other team mates have good **verbal and non-verbal** communication skills.
- In basketball, for example, you need to be able to respond to spoken instruction and advice from your teacher and team mates as you change from defence to attack and back again.

At times, non-verbal signals may be more effective than verbal signals. For example, when being marked tightly in attack in basketball, if you can signal (raising you arm, moving to the side, cutting and running to the basket) this can work better than calling for the ball as opponents will be unaware of non-verbal signals, but would hear and react to verbal signals.

Top-Tip

Physical qualities (cardiorespiratory, muscular endurance, speed, strength, power, flexibility) and personal qualities (determination, courage and self-confidence) are important when analysing tactics.

Tactics 2

Tactics [Credit Level Extension]

When analysing different tactics it is important to consider whether the skills included in different tactics are effective. It could be that the decision-making associated with the tactic is effective, but the skills required for completing the tactic are not. This is why you require analysis of performance before, during and after an activity.

Football example – zonal marking in defense

- Zonal marking is a method of defending in football. When using this tactic players take responsibility for an area of the pitch in defence (see diagram). This ensures that the team covers the width and depth of the pitch.

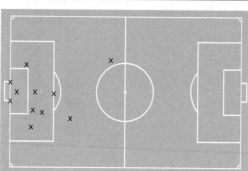

- The strength of zonal marking is that the team's defensive position forms a compact area around the most dangerous attacking positions. For zonal marking to work well the team needs to work well as a unit. When playing this type of defence no unmarked areas can be left for attacking players. It also helps if the goalkeeper is confident about coming out of his goal to collect crosses.

- When an attacking player is in possession the defensive team should react quickly and maintain the distance between team mates to ensure the defensive remains balanced. To do this well, players need to analyse what is happening around them. Players should be encouraged to give short verbal instructions to help each other.

- Communication is vital if players are to work effectively together. Zonal marking is an energy efficient way of defending as players do not move around unnecessarily. A disadvantage of zonal marking is that if players watch the ball and not the attacker, then the attacker can find space to create a scoring opportunity.

- When applying the different options in this defensive formation there are different principles of play, attacking tactics and skills to consider.

Principles of play	Defensive tactics – zone marking	Effective skills
Width Depth Delay	Team responsibilities – moving as a unit Awareness of attackers Make effective tactical decisions	Heading Quick reaction times Effective communication

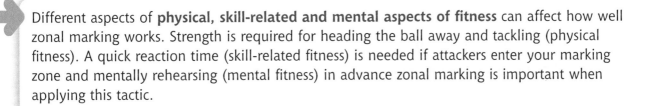

Different aspects of **physical, skill-related and mental aspects of fitness** can affect how well zonal marking works. Strength is required for heading the ball away and tackling (physical fitness). A quick reaction time (skill-related fitness) is needed if attackers enter your marking zone and mentally rehearsing (mental fitness) in advance zonal marking is important when applying this tactic.

Football example – Player marking in defense

Top-Tip
Decisions about your tactics are made before, during and after performance.

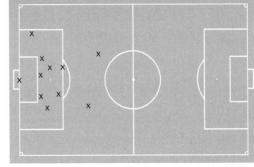

- With player marking each individual defender has responsibility for marking an attacking player. Effective defenders can use their positioning ability to win the ball from their opponents and prevent attacking players getting possession and shooting, passing or heading.

- Defenders should also have an overview of the positions of team mates. This makes it possible to advise team mates about their positions if, for example, an opponent moves behind them. In order to obtain such an overview, defenders need quick decision-making. One further advantage of player marking is that you can control who defenders mark. This makes it easy to match up players according to their strengths and weaknesses.

Top-Tip
Possessing good verbal and non-verbal communication skills is important when analysing tactics.

When applying the different options in this defensive formation there are different principles of play, attacking tactics and skills to consider.

Principles of play	Defensive tactics – player marking	Effective skills
Width	Player responsibilities	Heading
Depth	Positioning ability	Quick reaction times
Delay	Defenders selected to mark specific attackers	Effective communication

Quick Test

1. When do you analyse the effectiveness of a tactic?
2. What are the three principles of play?
3. Give an example of when non-verbal communication could work well in a team game.

Rules

Why do activities have rules?

- Activities have rules to ensure fair play and to ensure that activities run smoothly.
- There are different types of rules: safety rules, official / written or unofficial / unwritten rules and specific rules for different types of activities.
- The offside rule in football is an official / written rule.
- Kicking the ball out of play if a player is injured is an unofficial / unwritten rule in football.
- Unofficial / unwritten rules are expected to be followed so that activities can be played in fair and reasonable way.

Safety rules

- Wearing safety equipment can help you perform safely and to the best of your ability.
- Rules ensure safety through restricting players' movements and actions.

Activity	Rule		Reason for rule	Action taken if rule is broken
Tennis	The ball has to cross the net before you play the ball.		It would create an unfair advantage if you reached over the net to play the ball.	Point awarded to opponent
Hockey	When hitting in hockey the stick must be kept below shoulder height when near other players.		It is unsafe to swing the stick above shoulder height when near other players.	Free hit to defending team

Official / written or unofficial / unwritten rules are part of all the different categories of activities which are included within Standard Grade PE. Study the following examples.

CATEGORIES								
i Gymnastics	ii Dance	iii Water-based activities	iv Outdoor pursuits	v Individual activities: directly competitive	vi Individual activities: indirectly competitive	vii Team games: indoor	viii Team games: outdoor	ix Thematic study
Olympic	Modern	Life-saving	Hill-walking	Tennis	Athletics	Basketball	Rugby	Fitness
Official / written rules	Unofficial / unwritten rules	Official / written rules	Unofficial / unwritten rules	Official / written rules	Official / written rules	Official / written rules	Unofficial / unwritten rules	Official / written rules
There are official rules for floor sequences in Olympic gymnastics. These cover how long the time sequences last and the size of floor space.	It is expected (but not an official rule) that audiences are aware of when your performance is beginning.	There is a set of expected procedures you would follow in evaluating and carrying out a life-saving rescue.	It is a good idea (but not an official rule) to leave a safety note of your walking route.	There are official rules for scoring and serving within tennis.	In athletics there are objective rules for all track and field events.	In basketball there are official rules about travelling, shooting and contact between players.	In rugby as with many other games and activities it is usual to shake hands with your opponents at the end of the game	When completing a circuit there are set procedures to follow.

Specific rules for different activities

Specific rules define activities by noting where you are able to move and through different start and restart procedures. For example, in football all of the ball must cross the goal line for a goal to be awarded. In tennis, you need to win a set by two games, unless the set is decided by a tie-break.

In basketball attacking players are restricted from spending more than three seconds in the opposition's key when in possession of the ball. This means that attacking players need to move through and out of the key. If players stay in the key for more than three seconds possession is awarded to the opposing team.

Top-Tip
Official and unofficial rules ensure the smooth running of activities.

Quick Test

1. State three different types of rules.
2. Describe how wearing safety equipment can benefit participation.
3. Name an official rule which restricts player movements when attacking in basketball.

Answers **1.** There are safety rules, official / written or unofficial / unwritten rules and specific rules for different types of activities. **2.** By wearing the correct safety equipment you can focus on the demands of the activity, safe in the knowledge that you are well protected. **3.** The three-second rule.

Conduct and behaviour

Why is good conduct important?

Good conduct is important for the smooth running of activities. In the examples below note how for all the categories of activities which can be included within Standard Grade PE there are examples of how good conduct can benefit personal participation.

CATEGORIES								
i Gymnastics	ii Dance	iii Water-based activities	iv Outdoor pursuits	v Individual activities: directly competitive	vi Individual activities: indirectly competitive	vii Team games: indoor	viii Team games: outdoor	ix Thematic study
Rhythmic	Ethnic	Swimming	Skiing	Table tennis	Trampoline	Volleyball	Football	Fitness
Signal to audience when performance is ready to begin.	Consider other performers' suggestions when designing a dance.	Respect official rules by following instructions carefully at the start of a race.	Follow agreed rules for safe skiing on ski runs.	Conform with 'unofficial' rules by shaking hands at the end of the game.	When completing a pairs routine ensure partner is ready to begin.	Co-operate with team mates when defending and attacking.	Fair use of physical force when tackling.	Act responsibly when adjusting equipment when weight training.

In the examples below note how for all the categories of activities which can be included within Standard Grade PE there are examples of how good conduct can benefit non-participation roles.

CATEGORIES								
i Gymnastics	ii Dance	iii Water-based activities	iv Outdoor pursuits	v Individual activities: directly competitive	vi Individual activities: indirectly competitive	vii Team games: indoor	viii Team games: outdoor	ix Thematic study
Olympic	Modern	Canoeing	Orienteering	Badminton	Athletics	Basketball	Hockey	Fitness
Supporter	Tutor	Instructor	Timekeeper	Umpire	Starter	Referee	Umpire	Instructor
On the asymmetric bars I was supported to ensure that I did not over rotate.	My tutor provided me with feedback about whether my arms and legs were extended.	My instructor talked with me about the best way to complete the course.	The time-keeper in orienteering ensured that my time was correctly recorded.	The umpire in badminton observed the game closely and was fair to both teams when making decisions.	The starter explained the starting instructions carefully and this helped relax the competitors.	The referee signalled clearly to the recorders when players had committed a foul.	After the game the hockey umpire shook hands with both sets of players.	My fitness instructor explained the safety procedures for use with the cycling machine.

Top Tip
Good conduct and behaviour are closely linked to following the unwritten rules in many activities; for example, kicking the ball out of play in football, if a player is injured.

Quick Test

1. Explain why good conduct is important when participating in activities.
2. Explain why good conduct is important for non-participation roles in activities.

Answers 1. It enables activities to be participated in correctly; for example, safely and with consideration for other performers. 2. It enables activities to be participated in correctly; for example, by adhering to the formal rules of activities.

Scoring, adaptation and small-sided games

Scoring

Objective scoring systems are based on results; for example, considering which team has the highest score or measuring distances and time.

Examples of objective scoring

Activity		How winner is decided	Similar activities
Hockey		Most goals scored	Football
Rugby		Most points scored	Basketball, netball
Athletics (high jump)		Which athlete jumps the highest	Athletics (pole vault)
Athletics (triple jump)		Which athlete jumps the furthest	Athletics (long jump)
Athletics (discus)		Which athlete throws the furthest	Athletics (javelin; shot putt)
Athletics (800 m)		Which athlete runs the quickest	Athletics (100 m; 200 m; 400 m; 1500 m)

Subjective scoring systems are based on the opinions of judges.

Examples of subjective scoring

Activity		How winner is decided	Similar activities
Gymnastics (vault)		Best quality vault when judged against criteria	Gymnastics (floor; rings; parallel bars; beam)
Diving (spring board)		Best quality vault when judged against criteria	Diving (high board)

Adaptation

Activities can be adapted in many ways. For example, changes can be made to the rules, equipment, duration of activity and the size and layout of the playing area.

Activity		Adaptation	Benefits of adaptation
Basketball		Rules	Some formal time rules are relaxed so that play can develop more easily.
Athletics (discus)		Equipment (reduced size and weight)	Performer can throw the correct size and weight of discus for their age and ability.
Netball		Duration of activity	Time reductions can help players avoid becoming too tired.
Hockey		Size and layout of playing area	Cross pitch rather than full size games can ensure players become less tired during practice.

Small-sided games

Benefits of small-sided games

- More opportunity to transfer skills from practice to games
- More time and space to perform skills
- In football, for example, small-sided games of 5 v 5 or 7 v 7 players can be more suitable than 11 v 11 games.

Benefits of small-sided games when there are more attackers than defenders

- Easier for attacking team to practise attacking skills
- Chance for defending team to practise under increased pressure
- In hockey, for example, in a 6 v 4 game the six attacking players have an advantage and can score more easily.

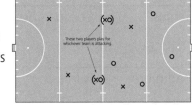

(reduced-size hockey pitch)

These two players play for whichever team is attacking.

Quick Test

1. Explain the difference between objective and subjective scoring.

2. Outline four ways in which activity could be adapted.

3. Explain why it is possible that a small-sided game can help transfer skills from practice to games.

Roles and responsibilities, personal qualities, physical qualities

Performing roles and responsibilities

When practising with other students your role will often involve helping other students. Being an effective opponent in a practice is one common way of recognising the importance of your responsibility.

Non-performing roles and responsibilities

By officiating in games you can take responsibility for the smooth running of activities in a non-performing way.

Personal qualities

Co-operation, fairness, concentration and determination are some of the most common personal qualities required in different activities.

Examples of personal qualities

Activity	Personal quality	Role		Reason for personal quality
Tennis	Co-operation	Performer		I co-operated with my doubles partner to make sure that we played well as a team.
Badminton	Fairness	Umpire		I had to ensure that the rules were applied fairly to each player as per the official rules of the game.
Orienteering	Concentration	Timekeeper		As competitors completed the course I recorded accurately each performer's time.
Trampoline	Determination	Performer		When completing a back somersault for the first time determination was required.

Physical qualities

Co-ordination, speed, control and cardiorespiratory endurance are some of the most common personal qualities required in different activities.

Examples of physical qualities

Activity	Physical quality	Role		Reason for physical quality
Volleyball	Co-ordination	Setter		When setting in volleyball I needed control when relaxing and extending my arm and leg movements.
Netball	Speed	Wing defence		When playing as a wing defence in netball I needed to move quickly to cover the movements of other players.
Hockey	Control	Midfield		When push passing in hockey I needed to have good control of the ball and my body movements.
Basketball	Cardio-respiratory endurance	Referee		Having to be on court for the entire game meant that I needed good cardiorespiratory endurance.

Top Tip
Effective participation depends upon having a mix of physical and personal qualities.

Quick Test

1. Name four personal qualities.
2. Name four physical qualities.

Answers 1. Co-operation, fairness, concentration and determination. 2. Co-ordination, speed, control and cardiorespiratory endurance.

23

Oxygen transport system

How the oxygen transport works – four key points

- The main aim of the oxygen transport system is to help you exercise.
- As you increase oxygen intake during exercise (by breathing in) you can participate and train in more demanding ways.
- The lungs, heart, blood and muscles all play an important part in the oxygen transport system.
- The **respiratory** and **circulatory** systems work together to provide muscles with oxygen, which enables you to exercise.

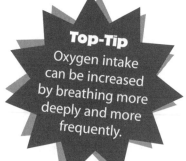

Top-Tip
Oxygen intake can be increased by breathing more deeply and more frequently.

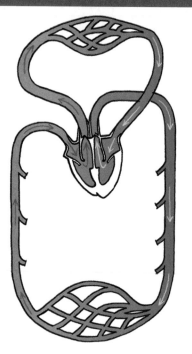

The benefits of training – six key points

- Regular exercise is very good for the heart and lungs: it increases the size of the heart.
- This enables more blood to be pushed around the body following a contraction of the heart muscles.
- This lowers the heart rate.
- The lower your heart rate the fitter you are.
- By improving your oxygen transport system you can raise your anaerobic threshold.
- This means you can work aerobically for a longer time and at a higher level of intensity.

An 800m runner who aims to complete their run in 2 minutes 30 seconds to 3 minutes would benefit from an effective oxygen transport system as this would enable them to work aerobically for a longer time and at a quicker speed.

Different levels of oxygen intake during physical activity – four key points

- The size of your lungs increases as you exercise and this provides the body with more oxygen through deeper and more frequent breathing.
- The more oxygen you can take into your lungs the greater will be your capacity for exercise.
- This can be measured through breathing tests which calculate your maximal oxygen uptake or VO2 max during a minute of exercise.
- At rest you usually breathe about 12–15 times per minute, but this can increase to 30–40 times per minute when exercising.

Effects of lactic acid / oxygen debt

Key points	Activities where lactic acid / oxygen debt is a key consideration
- If you perform for long time intervals it is often difficult for your breathing to supply enough oxygen to working muscles. - This leads to a build up of lactic acid in your muscles, which will eventually force you to slow down. - This is because your muscles will have fatigue. Sometimes, as well, cramp can occur. - Lactic acid can only be removed with oxygen. Until more oxygen arrives by deep and frequent breathing you will suffer from oxygen debt. - For these reasons it is beneficial to train regularly so that working muscles can get used to the demands of training. - It is also worthwhile to try to delay the build up in lactic acid occurring.	

Quick Test

1. What is the main aim of the oxygen transport system?

2. Which two systems work together to provide muscles with oxygen?

3. Describe two advantages of increasing your anaerobic threshold.

4. How often do you breathe when exercising?

5. Explain how fatigue occurs.

Answers 1. To help you exercise. 2. The respiratory and circulatory systems. 3. It means you can work aerobically for a longer time and at a higher level of intensity. 4. Usually around 30–40 breaths per minute. 5. Fatigue occurs when it is difficult for your breathing to supply enough oxygen to working muscles.

Body structure, joints and movement of a hinge joint

Body structure – four key points

- Your **skeleton** supports your body, protects vital organs (heart, lungs), produces blood within longer bones such as the thigh (femur) and enables movements to occur.
- Muscles are attached to the bones of the skeleton by a connective tissue known as a **tendon**.
- **Cartilage** acts a buffer to protect bones.
- **Ligaments** join bones to other bones and help provide stability in joints by preventing over-stretching and over-twisting.

Muscle functions and groups of muscles

Elbow joint

As the triceps muscle relaxes and lengthens, the biceps muscle contracts and shortens. This allows the elbow joint to flex. When the elbow joint is required to extend the opposite applies: the biceps muscle relaxes and lengthens and the triceps muscle contracts and shortens.

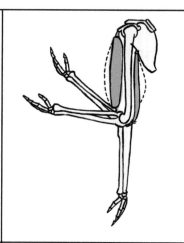

Knee joint

As the knee joint flexes, the muscles at the front of the thigh (quadriceps) relax and lengthen while the muscles at the back of the thigh (hamstrings) contract and shorten. When the knee joint is required to extend the opposite applies: the front thigh muscles contract and shorten and the back thigh muscles relax and lengthen.

Top-Tip
Muscles function by working in pairs or groups.

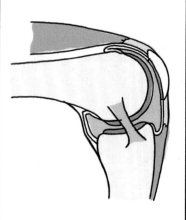

Joints

Type of joint	Where found		Range of movement	Explanation
Hinge	Knee		Movement is possible in one direction (plane) only in an open and close movement.	The opening and closing of the knee joint enables a powerful shot in football.
	Elbow			The opening and closing of the elbow joint enables a powerful shot putt.
Ball and socket	Hips		Movement is possible in all directions.	Holding this balance on the beam in gymnastics is helped by the range of movement possible in the hip joint.
	Shoulder			Rotation of the shoulder joint enables a powerful overarm serve in volleyball to take place.

Top-Tip
Ball and socket and hinge joints are examples of freely moveable joints.

Joints [Credit grade extension]

For different actions, try to observe and describe the order of joint movements. For example, if you study the three pictures of the javelin thrower below you can see how the shoulder (ball and socket) joint leads the action (first two pictures) in establishing a strong pull position. The elbow (hinge) joint then helps keep the arm long during the throw. Observing and describing in this way will help develop your evaluation abilities.

CREDIT

Quick Test

1. What to ligaments do?

2. What type of joints are the elbow and knee?

3. Name one advantage of observing and describing the order of joint movements.

Answers 1. Ligaments join bones to other bones and help provide stability in joints by preventing over-stretching and over-twisting. 2. Hinge joints. 3. It will help develop your evaluation abilities.

Physical fitness: cardiorespiratory endurance

Introduction

- To improve your cardiorespiratory endurance you need to work for long intervals at a low level of intensity. You need a lot of oxygen to supply working muscles. This means you will be working aerobically.
- Anaerobic activity, by contrast, occurs when there is a shortage of oxygen. When you are working to improve your anaerobic fitness you need to work for short intervals at a high level of intensity.
- Aerobic or anaerobic activity leads to differences in **your pulse**, **breathing** and **body temperature**.

		Pulse	Above average, 120-170 beats per minute
Aerobic activity		Breathing	Above average with steady rhythm (increase from resting rate of 12 breaths a minute to 30 breaths a minute approx.)
		Body temperature	Above average, as regular exercise raises body temperature
		Pulse	From rest to high, 180–200 beats per minute in a short time
Anaerobic activity		Breathing	Little effect during exercise as exercise lasts for short time. Frequent deep breathing needed for recovery
		Body temperature	Little effect as exercise lasts for short time

Top-Tip

Cardiorespiratory endurance is the ability of the whole body to work continuously.

The effects of cardiorespiratory endurance on performance

Advantages of good cardiorespiratory endurance

- In activities where you take part for relatively long periods of time improved cardiorespiratory endurance provides you with the chance to perform better.
- This is because you are able to carry out skills and concentrate better if you are able to cope with the endurance demands of activities.
- When you are tired (fatigued) mistakes are more likely to occur.

Top-Tip
Remember aerobic = with oxygen, anaerobic = without oxygen.

Hockey	Rugby union	Life-saving
Good cardiorespiratory endurance means that my skill level remains high throughout the entire game.	Good cardiorespiratory endurance means that I can make offensive attacking runs throughout the entire game.	Good cardiorespiratory endurance means that I can complete long demanding rescues.

Measuring cardiorespiratory endurance

The 20 m shuttle run test, the Harvard Step Test and the 12-minute running test are all tests for measuring your cardiorespiratory endurance.

20 m shuttle run test	12-minute running test	Harvard Step Test
The test measures how far you can run as the time allowable for you to complete your 20 m runs gradually decreases.	The test measures the distance you can run in 12 minutes. The distance around the athletics track is 400 m.	The test uses your recovery rate to calculate your level of cardiorespiratory endurance.

Top-Tip
When training to improve cardiorespiratory endurance keep exercises simple.

Quick Test

1. What will be your pulse rate when working aerobically?
2. What will be your pulse rate when working anaerobically?
3. Name two advantages of good cardiorespiratory endurance.

Answers 1. 120–170 beats per minute. 2. 180–200 beats per minute. 3. It enables you to participate for relatively long periods of time and to carry out skills and concentrate better.

Physical fitness: cardiorespiratory endurance

Monitoring the effectiveness of cardiorespiratory endurance training

- You can monitor your progress when exercising by checking your pulse regularly.
- Remember that a simple way to check your heart rate during exercise is to pause and take your pulse for 6 seconds. Multiply your total for 6 seconds by 10 to get your heart rate per minute.
- Pulse rate information is useful for working out your resting pulse rate, your highest pulse rate and your recovery rate after exercise.
- Pulse rate information is also useful for working out whether you are working aerobically or anaerobically. This involves working out your **training zone** for aerobic exercise.

How to calculate your training zone

The harder you exercise, the faster your heart beats. This means that your maximum heart rate is an indicator of how you are exercising and of whether you are using your aerobic or anaerobic energy system.

A formula calculates your training zone. You subtract your age from the maximum heart rate of 220 beats per minute. For Example:

Maximum Heart Rate 220 – 15 = 205
60% of 205 = 123
85% of 205 = 174

If you are 15 years old your training zone is between 122 and 173 beats per minute. The formula for calculating your training zone uses 60% and 85% of maximum heart rate to work out the lower and upper training thresholds of when you are training effectively for cardiorespiratory endurance and in your **aerobic training zone**.

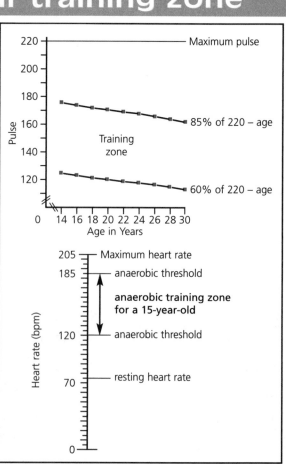

Monitoring your pulse rate during training

Training to develop anaerobic endurance

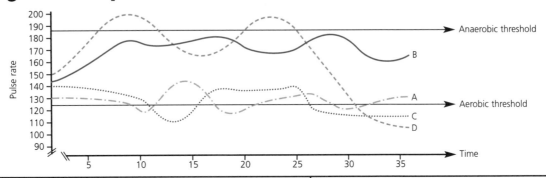

Pulse rate Profile	Work rate profile	Rest and recovery profile
A	**Limited effectiveness** Has three periods of work when the pulse is just above the minimum limit for the aerobic training zone.	The work to rest interval is reasonable, however during each rest phase the pulse is lower than necessary for effective training.
B	**Highly effective** The pulse is within the aerobic training zone for the whole training period (30 mins). The pulse comes close to the upper limit before slowly lowering to more manageable levels.	The work to rest interval excellent, not too short to be ineffective, not too long for pulse to drop out of aerobic training.
C	**Limited effectiveness** During the beginning and middle part of the training period the intensity of the work level is very good.	The work to rest interval is poor, as the two rest interval periods (between 12-15 minutes and from 26-30 minutes) are too long and the pulse drops out of the aerobic training zone.
D	**Limited effectiveness** The pulse rate is promising at the beginning, however on two occasions the intensity of work is too demanding and the level of exercise is using the anaerobic rather than the aerobic energy system.	The work to rest interval is reasonable, however, the effect of working above the aerobic threshold is that it becomes too difficult for recovery to take place. The effect is that the pulse drops below the minimum necessary for effective training by the end of the training period.

Quick Test

1. Why is pulse rate information useful?

2. If you are 15 years old, how many heart beats per minute is your training zone?

Physical fitness: muscular endurance

Introduction

- Using the same muscle groups repeatedly over long periods of time requires muscular endurance.
- To improve your muscular endurance you need to work muscle groups for long intervals at a relatively low level of intensity.
- Poor muscular endurance leads to fatigue and your muscles will feel tired and heavy.

The effects of muscular endurance on performance

For many activities you require good muscle tone in major muscle groups for effective performance.

In volleyball you require good muscular endurance in the leg muscles to be able to jump high to block opposition spikes repeatedly during games. If your muscles become fatigued you will jump less effectively.	In basketball you require good muscular endurance in the arm muscles to be able to keep your arms raised throughout the game when defending. If your muscles become fatigued it will become increasingly difficult to keep your arms raised.

Top-Tip
Muscular endurance is the ability of muscles to work continuously.

Muscular endurance

Measuring muscular endurance

There are various tests for measuring muscular endurance.

The bent knee sit-up test is an effective test for measuring the muscular endurance of the abdominal (stomach) muscles.	Squat thrusts are an effective way of measuring the muscular endurance of the leg muscles.

Training to improve muscular endurance

Overloading muscles in training will provide more oxygen for muscle groups.

Circuit training is one effective way of improving muscular endurance. A circuit typically includes the following types of exercises: sit-ups; burpees; press-ups; dips; shuttle runs and step-ups. Each of the exercises involved in the circuit is particularly useful for different muscles groups.

Weight training is a further effective way of improving muscular endurance and involves low weights and high repetitions as the muscular work is endurance based. Weight training exercises such as upright row and squats are often included in weight training circuits

Quick Test

1. What happens if you have poor muscular endurance?

2. Name two tests / exercises which are effective for measuring muscular endurance.

3. Name six exercises which might be part of a circuit-training programme.

Answers **1.** It leads to fatigue and your muscles will feel tired and heavy. **2.** The bent knee sit-up test, and squat thrusts. **3.** Sit-ups; burpees; press-ups; dips; shuttle runs and step-ups.

Physical fitness: muscular endurance

Monitoring the effectiveness of muscular endurance training

- When training, it is useful to measure your initial level of muscular endurance in different exercises when taking part in different activities.
- This enables you to set challenging but achievable targets.
- It also enables you to calculate how best to overload your training progressively, for example by completing more exercises.

Training to improve muscular endurance

Progressive overload for muscular endurance would usually involve completing exercises for longer periods of time (duration) or more repetitions of exercises (frequency). You could also decrease the rest intervals between sets of exercises.

In the example below note how the weight training programme in week 8 is more demanding than the programme in week 4 and week 1. Progressive overload has been added by increasing the weight lifted between weeks 1 and 4, and by increasing the number of repetitions of exercises between weeks 4 and 8.

I need muscular endurance in my upper body so that I can paddle for long periods of time without tiring.

3 circuits of the following circuit with 2 minutes' rest between each set.		
Week 1 Weight training		
Exercise	Weight lifted	Repetitions
Bench press	15 kg	20
Upright row	5 kg	20
Pull down	10 kg	20
Week 4 Weight training		
Exercise	Weight lifted	Repetitions
Bench press	20 kg	20
Upright row	8 kg	20
Pull down	12 kg	20
Week 8 Weight training		
Exercise	Weight lifted	Repetitions
Bench press	20 kg	25
Upright row	8 kg	25
Pull down	12 kg	25

Effective training is based on making correct planning decisions. Study the two examples below and identify the key steps which are made to ensure training is effective.

Key Steps		Planning decisions
Activity: Volleyball **Position:** Spiker / blocker **Key Step 1:** Measure initial level of muscular endurance **Key Step 2:** Set challenging but achievable targets **Key Step 3:** Decide on appropriate form of training **Key Step 4:** Calculate how best to progressively overload your training **Key Step 5:** Evaluate whether performance in volleyball has improved		Complete squat thrusts (maximum number possible within 30 seconds) to measure the muscular endurance of the leg muscles. Block higher percentage of opposition spikes during games. Circuit training based on inclusion of leg exercises – bench jumps, burpees and shuttle runs. Increase the number of repetitions within a set to increase the duration of exercises. Analyse whether a higher percentage of opposition spikes during games were blocked following completion of training programme.

Key Steps		Planning decisions
Activity: Basketball **Position:** Guard **Key Step 1:** Measure initial level of muscular endurance **Key Step 2:** Set challenging but achievable targets **Key Step 3:** Decide on appropriate form of training **Key Step 4:** Calculate how best to progressively overload your training **Key Step 5:** Evaluate whether performance in basketball has improved		Complete the bent arm hang test to measure the muscular endurance of the upper body and arm muscles. While defending, increase ability to keep arms outstretched and extended when necessary without tiring. Weight training based on inclusion of upper body and arm exercises such as bench press, upright row and pull down. Increase the number of repetitions within a set to increase the duration of exercises. Analyse whether improved body posture was evident when defending in games following completion of training programme.

The effects of increased muscular endurance on the body

- Improved muscular endurance should ensure that you have better muscle tone and posture.
- This often means that you are able to complete skills more effectively (improved control and fluency), especially when you begin to get tired.

Quick Test

1. Explain why it is useful to measure your initial level of muscular endurance in different exercises before your training programme begins.
2. Explain two methods for adding progressive overload to your training programme.

Answers **1.** It enables you to set challenging but achievable targets. **2.** Progressive overload can be added by completing exercises for longer periods of time (duration) or more repetitions of exercises (frequency).

Physical fitness: strength

Introduction

- The three main types of strength are: static; explosive and dynamic.
- Different activities require different types of strength.
- To improve your strength you need to work muscle groups for short intervals at a relatively high level of intensity.

The effects of strength on performance

Static strength	Explosive strength	Dynamic strength
In rugby you need static strength in certain scrums to hold the scrum steady. This prevents the other team's forwards from driving you backwards.	When throwing the javelin you need explosive strength as throwing the javelin involves using maximum energy in a single action.	When sprinting in swimming, for example, when completing a 100 m front crawl race, you need dynamic strength to work continuously the major muscles of the arm and shoulder.

Measuring your strength

Static strength		You squeeze as hard as possible for a few seconds.
Explosive strength		You complete a two-footed jump and measure the distance from the marked start line to the back of your furthest back foot on landing.
Dynamic strength		These exercises are similar to those used for measuring muscular endurance. For measuring dynamic strength the exercises would usually last for a shorter training time.

Training to improve strength

Weight training is an effective way to improve all types of strength. Exercises will vary according to the type of strength requiring improvement (static, explosive and dynamic).

When completing a weight training programme you need to consider how many **repetitions** and **sets** of different exercises you will complete. For example, you might complete ten repetitions of an exercise on three occasions in a set.

- Moving a heavy weight a few times increases static strength.
- Moving a medium weight very fast improves explosive strength.
- Moving a light weight improves dynamic strength initially (and muscular endurance if continued for a longer time).

Safety advice: Take care to ensure that you avoid placing any unnecessary strain on your muscles when weight training. Any increases in weight should be gradual.

Monitoring strength training

For monitoring strength training it is useful to ensure the type of muscle action (isometric, isokinetic) links to the muscle groups being exercised and to the methods being used.

Isometric exercises are used when muscles are required to be stable and still. This would be useful in dance, for example, when strength is required in balances.

Isokinetic exercises are used when muscles require control through a range of movements. During these types of exercise the amount of muscular force increases and decreases as movement occurs, for example, in football the rapid extension of the lower leg during the kicking motion is necessary.

The effects of increased strength on the body

Improved strength should mean that you have the capacity to complete actions which link physical and skill-related aspects of fitness.

When defending in basketball players require upper and lower body strength to ensure that they can adopt a strong posture when defending.	The defender needs good strength and dynamic balance.
Being able to complete a long pass in hockey requires upper and lower body strength.	The hockey player needs good strength and co-ordination.

Quick Test

1. Name three main types of strength.
2. Fill in the missing words: to improve your strength you need to work ------ groups for ------ intervals at a relatively high level of ---.
3. Name a test for measuring explosive strength.
4. What is the difference between isometric and isokinetic exercises.

Answers 1. Static, explosive and dynamic. 2. Muscles, short, intensity. 3. Standing long jump test. 4. Isometric exercises are used when muscles are required to be stable and still. Isokinetic exercises require control through a range of movements.

Physical fitness: speed

Introduction

- Speed is the ability to cover a distance or perform a movement in a short time.
- To improve your speed you need to work muscle groups for short intervals at a relatively high level of intensity.

The effects of speed on performance

In many team and individual activities speed is required by the whole body. On other occasions speed is required by only part of the body.

Measuring speed

There are various tests for measuring speed, most of which involve sprinting over relatively short distances such as 10 m and 20 m. Speed tests can be easily set up.

Training to improve speed

Speed training involves you using anaerobic (without oxygen) energy most. For this reason you need to ensure that your rest and recovery time is long enough. This often means that you would work for one repetition of an exercise and rest for four times as long. For example, sprinting for five seconds and resting for twenty seconds.

Top-Tip

Make sure you allow an adequate recovery time when training to improve speed. This will avoid fatigue and the build up of lactic acid in muscles.

Monitoring the effectiveness of speed training

When training, it is useful to measure your initial level of speed in different exercises and when taking part in different activities. Progressive overload for speed would usually involve completing exercises for short periods of time (duration) with repetitions of exercises (frequency) following adequate time for rest and recovery. Rest is necessary as it allows time for the reduction of oxygen debt and the removal of lactic acid.

The effects of increased speed on the body

Improved speed should mean that you have the capacity to complete actions which link physical and skill-related aspects of fitness.

The discus thrower requires leg speed to ensure that they can turn quickly and build up speed before throwing the discus.		The discus thrower needs good speed and dynamic balance to produce an excellent throw.
The cricketer requires whole body speed so that they can move quickly into position to play the shot they have chosen.		The cricketer needs good speed and co-ordination to play an attacking shot.
The 100m sprinter requires speed to move the arms and legs quickly to generate and maintain a fast running action.		The sprinter needs good speed and a quick reaction time to run a fast time.
The badminton player needs good speed and agility to reach and return the shuttlecock.		The badminton player requires speed to move quickly to reach and return the shuttlecock.

Quick Test

1. Define speed.

2. What type of energy is required for speed training – aerobic or anaerobic?

3. What is the likely work to rest ratio for speed training?

4. Why is rest necessary in speed training?

Answers 1. Speed is the ability to cover a distance or perform a movement in a short time. **2.** Anaerobic. **3.** One repetition of work followed by four times the work interval for recovery time. **4.** Rest is necessary as it allows time for the reduction of oxygen debt and the removal of lactic acid.

Physical fitness: power

Introduction

- Power is the combination of strength and speed.
- To improve your power you need to work muscle groups for short intervals at a high level of intensity.

The effects of power on performance

Power is required in many activities, for example, the jumping action when blocking in volleyball and completing a slap hit in hockey. Power is needed, along with effective technique, in different kicking and striking actions, for example, kicking for distance in rugby and batting in softball.

Measuring your power

There are various tests for measuring power. In the standing high jump or standing long jump tests, explosive power is needed as you are trying to jump as high or as far as possible from a standing start. In both of these tests explosive power is created by powerful leg muscles and by gaining additional height or distance by swinging your arms.

Vertical jump test

Stretch you arms above your head and mark the height with your fingertips. Then stand sideways to the marking board and jump as high as possible and mark the height with your fingertips. Measure the distance between the two marks.

Standing long jump

From behind the take-off line, complete a two-footed jump and measure the distance from the take-off line to the rearmost mark of your landing.

Training to improve power

Explosive power is best improved by increasing strength in the main muscles used for different activities and by exercises requiring speed.

Exercise	Maximum	Weight used for power exercise	Repetition
Squats	80 kg	60 kg	5
Bench press	60 kg	45 kg	5
Bicep curl	20 kg	15 kg	5

Power [Credit Grade Extension]

Monitoring the effectiveness of power training

When you monitor power you have to consider the size of the force applied as well as the speed of the force applied. When shooting in football, leg power enables you to move your foot quickly so that you can apply a large force on the ball.

To replicate the demands of power in training would usually involve adding progressive overload by completing exercises for very short periods of time (duration) followed by adequate time for rest and recovery. As your training progresses, you would add to the intensity of exercises, for example, by increasing weight if weight training. For speed-related work decreasing rest times would be suitable as a method of increasing the intensity of exercises.

The effects of increased power on the body

Improved power should mean that you have the capacity to complete actions which link physical and skill-related aspects of fitness.

In basketball, the jump shooter needs to bend their knees and powerfully straighten them and jump upwards to shoot.		The jump shooter needs power and dynamic balance to ensure that they jump only upwards when shooting and not upwards and forwards.
The javelin thrower in athletics requires to pull their arm back fully, then build up speed when pulling arm forward, so that explosive power is generated when they throw the javelin.		The javelin thrower needs power and co-ordination to throw the javelin a long distance.
The line out jumper in rugby union bends their knees and powerfully straightens them and jumps upwards to catch the ball.		The rugby player needs power and reaction time to ensure that they catch the ball when they are at the top of their jump.
The long jumper in athletics requires speed and strength at the take-off to jump a long distance.		The long jumper needs good speed and agility to transfer from running quickly to beginning a jumping action.

Quick Test

1. Define power.

2. Name two tests for measuring power.

Answers 1. Power is the combination of strength and speed. 2. The vertical jump and standing long jump test.

Physical fitness: flexibility

Introduction

- Flexibility is the range of movement across a joint.
- Having good flexibility reduces the chances of straining or pulling muscles.
- Controlled stretching exercises can be used to maintain and improve flexibility.

The effects of flexibility on performance

Flexibility is required in many activities.

When hurdling in athletics the hurdler needs hip flexibility in particular, as this will help the hurdler clear the hurdles with minimum effort and maximum efficiency.	
The swimmer needs back flexibility to help when pushing off and arm and shoulder flexibility to produce a wide range of movement during the back crawl stroke. This will help make the swimming stroke more effective.	

There are two types of flexibility: static and dynamic flexibility.

Static flexibility is necessary when you are holding a balance in gymnastics.	
Dynamic flexibility requires flexibility for a short time within your overall performance. For example, the high jumper requires dynamic flexibility when arching their back during their jump.	

Measuring your flexibility

There are various tests for measuring flexibility. Two examples are the 'sit-and-reach test' which measures flexibility in the hip joint and in the muscles at the back of the thigh (hamstrings), and the 'trunk extension test' which measures the flexibility of the lower back.

Training to improve flexibility

- When training to improve flexibility you stretch and move joints just beyond the point at which you feel resistance.
- Flexibility is affected by the type of joint and muscle attachment.
- Flexibility is limited by ligaments which hold joints in place. The elasticity of tendons which attach muscles to bones and joints also limits the degree of flexibility possible.
- Exercises to maintain and improve flexibility are usually either **static** or **active** exercises.
- In static exercises you hold a stretched position for a few seconds.
- With active (ballistic) stretching exercises you use movement to move a body part at a joint.

Flexibility [Credit Grade Extension]

Monitoring the effectiveness of flexibility training

- When you monitor flexibility you have to consider the joints and muscles where flexibility is required.
- Next you need to consider the type of static and dynamic stretching exercises which would best benefit your performance.
- Ensure that you complete stretching exercises for the front of the thigh (quadriceps) and that you also complete stretching exercises for the back of the thigh (hamstring) muscles.

CREDIT

The effects of increased flexibility on the body

Improved flexibility should mean that you have the capacity to complete actions which link physical and skill-related aspects of fitness.

In gymnastics, the gymnast needs good hip and leg flexibility in order to perform splits leap on the beam.		The gymnast needs flexibility and dynamic balance to ensure that they can perform challenging splits leap on the beam.
The dancer needs flexibility in all the major joints in order to perform linked flowing movements.		The dancer needs flexibility and co-ordination in order to complete movements with control, fluency and in the correct order.

Quick Test

1. Define Flexibility.

2. Name two types of flexibility.

3. Why is resistance important for the effective completion of flexibility stretching exercises?

Top-Tip
When training to improve flexibility it is important that you stretch forward carefully and not in a sudden way.

Answers 1. Flexibility is the range of movement across a joint. 2. Static and dynamic flexibility. 3. When resistance begins it indicates the point where stretching should stop.

Skill-related fitness: co-ordination and agility

Introduction

- Co-ordination is the ability to control movements smoothly and fluently in the correct order.
- To perform in a co-ordinated way, groups of muscles work in a specific sequence to create effective movements.

Good co-ordination can benefit technique. For example, when completing a smash in badminton, linking co-ordination with power can ensure that your smash is successful.

Skill-related fitness: co-ordination [Credit Grade Extension]

As your co-ordination improves, you are able to move your joints and muscles in the correct order. This leads to improvements in your hand and eye co-ordination, for example when catching a ball. Improved co-ordination also improves control and fluency. This is important when completing a handspring vault in gymnastics, as it enables the legs to stay extended as they overtake the arms with both hands striking the mat together and legs landing together.

Skill-related fitness: agility

Introduction

Agility is the ability to move the body quickly and precisely.

The dancer needs agility to change direction and shape with controlled fluent movements.	
The volleyball player needs agility in order to be able to move quickly and lower their centre of gravity. This helps them to get behind the ball and maintain control of the shot.	
The footballer needs agility to maintain close control of the ball when dribbling.	

Skill-related fitness: agility [Credit Grade Extension]

CREDIT

As your agility improves you can make ever quicker changes in direction. In many activities this would be an advantage, for example, in rugby union when swerving past a defender.

Initially, you would run directly at the defender. As they begin to commit to tackling you begin to change your angle of run by arcing away from the defender.

By leaning away from the tackler and running as quickly as possible you increase your chances of getting past the defender.

Quick Test

1. Define co-ordination.
2. Define agility.

Skill-related fitness: balance and reaction time

Balance – introduction

- Balance is the ability to retain the centre of gravity over your base of support.
- Balancing requires the control of different groups of muscles.
- Static balances such as a handstand in gymnastics require you to hold a balance, while dynamic balances require you to maintain balance under constantly changing conditions.

Static balance

Dynamic balance

Balance [Credit Grade Extension]

As your static balance improves you are more likely to be able to show fine motor control and good control of your strength and body weight. In the handstand balance you move from using large body movements to complete the balance using fine body movements which helps improve your stability.

CREDIT

As your dynamic balance improves you are more likely to be able to show control in demanding situations. For example, when kayaking you can constantly adjust your dynamic balance as you paddle through different currents and water conditions in order to remain in balance.

Reaction time – introduction

- Reaction time is the time taken between the recognition of a signal and the start of a movement response. It is linked to speed.

- If you are returning a serve in tennis you need to respond quickly. A fast reaction time and quick court movements would benefit your performance. For example, if you were returning a 50 mph serve you would only have 1.1 seconds to react.

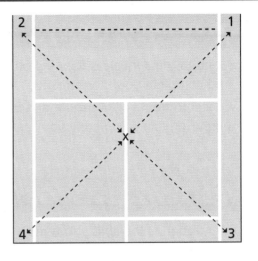

Reaction time [Credit Grade Extension]

As your reaction time improves you are likely to think and respond more quickly. This should lead to fewer errors in movement and more time to make decisions. For example, in a line out in rugby union, practice between the thrower and the jumpers and supporters should ensure that you are able to secure possession. This will be more difficult to achieve when the opposing team have the throw in, as you will have less time to respond and time your jump accordingly.

CREDIT

Quick Test

1. Define balance.

2. What is the difference between a static and dynamic balance?

3. Define reaction time.

Answers 1. Balance is the ability to retain the centre of gravity over your base of support. 2. Static balances require you to hold a balance, while dynamic balances require you to maintain balance under constantly changing conditions. 3. Reaction time is the time taken between the recognition of a signal and the start of a movement response.

Mental fitness

Introduction

- Mental fitness involves focusing on those factors which help you prepare and complete your performance.
- Concentration, confidence and motivation are all important factors in preparing and completing your performance.

Mental fitness – concentration

Concentration is the ability to remain focused when performing.

Volleyball example

To perform to a high level you need to pay attention to important parts of your performance. For example, when 'setting' in volleyball you need to focus on certain factors. These include the flight of the ball and the movements of your team mates. It is also useful if you can look to see if the other team has players getting ready to 'block' at the net.

Mental fitness – confidence

Confidence is a positive state for mind; a belief in yourself that you can perform successfully.

Football example

In football, if you are confident about your ability it will help you to believe that you can retain close control of the ball and dribble past defenders.

Mental fitness – motivation

Motivation is your level of desire to succeed. Internal motivation is your own 'internal' level of desire to succeed. External motivation occurs when your involvement in an activity is for reasons apart from simply participating.

Orienteering example

When competing in orienteering I became very tired. However, I wanted to succeed as I had trained hard for the competition, so I kept going right to the finishing line.

Mental fitness – combined example

lap 1   laps 2–3   lap 4

In a 1500m race in athletics it is a good idea to think ahead to how you are going to cope with tiredness. You can mentally prepare in a positive way by breaking the whole race down into a series of smaller steps. Then as you achieve the smaller steps, such as 'coping with the opening lap' (for example, runner X below is quite content that she is in third place in lap 1) and 'keeping up with the leaders in the middle laps of the race', you feel good about your performance and can keep going to the finish in a fast time. By mentally preparing ahead like this you are better placed to do well.

Your mental preparation is based on **concentration** (watching other runners closely during the race and remembering individual lap times), **confidence** (you are comfortable running behind the leader during opening and middle parts of the race) and your **motivation** (desire to win).

Mental fitness [Credit Grade Extension]

Your mental preparation is likely to be high if you feel safe about what you are doing. This is especially the case in some activities like gymnastics when you are practising new and often complex skills for the first time. Ensuring that there are adequate safety mats in place and often a class mate or teacher to support your movements, as necessary, can help improve your confidence and overall mental preparation.

Mental preparation is also helped by
- selecting a quiet area, away from the competition / performance area
- establishing a clear picture in your mind of quality performance
- breaking the performance down into smaller parts
- being positive, imagining doing well.

Quick Test

1. Name three aspects of mental fitness which are important in preparing and completing your performance.
2. Define concentration.
3. Explain the difference between internal and external motivation.

Warm up and warm down

Introduction

The aim of an effective warm up is to gradually get your whole body prepared for work. This will ensure that you prevent injury to muscles, tendons and ligaments.

Four key stages are involved in an effective warm up. These are:

1	Increase your pulse rate by raising the blood flow to the muscles. This can be achieved through aerobic exercise such as jogging, building up to light running for a few minutes. After this exercise you should have raised your body temperature and increased joint mobility.	
2	Complete stretching exercises for the large muscle groups. Stretching exercises should last a further few minutes. After this exercise your muscles should be supple.	
3	Refresh a few specific skill-related practices for the activity you are participating in. For example, if the activity is basketball, practise a few lay up shots for a further few minutes. After this exercise you should be familiar with some of the performance skills involved in the activity.	
4	Prepare your mind for the activity ahead. You might wish to note these down. After this exercise you should be able to focus on your performance improvement objectives.	

Top-Tip
Take care to ensure that you avoid placing any unnecessary strain on your muscles, joints and tendons when warming up.

Warm up

Badminton example

Stage 1: Reflecting the four key stages mentioned earlier, an effective warm up for badminton would begin with some gentle jogging and light running for a few minutes around the court.

 Stage 2: Next, you would complete some stretching exercises. An important consideration for a racquet game would be ensuring that some upper body exercises were included. For this reason you might include various arm swinging and side stretching exercises.

You might also include lunges where you step forward and bend the knee of the front leg and lower the trunk into a deep position. This exercise can be practised with or without the badminton racquet.

Stage 3: Next, you could complete a few specific skill-related practices. In the first practice the aim is to run, change direction, and stay in balance when moving through using precise footwork. In practice 2 the intention is to practise (simulate) different types of shot when at the different corners of the badminton court.

Stage 4: Prepare your mind for the activity ahead.

Warm down

- The purpose of the warm down (or cool down) is to help your body to recover after exercise and for your heart rate to decrease slowly.
- It should start with jogging or light running. This will help the blood circulation to carry more oxygen to the muscles, which in turn will help reduce muscle stiffness as lactic acid is removed more quickly. This exercise should last a few minutes.
- Complete your warm down with some stretching. This will help keep muscles supple.

Quick Test

1. What is the first key stage of a warm up?
2. What is the second key stage of a warm up?
3. What is the third key stage of a warm up?
4. What is the fourth key stage of a warm up?
5. What is the purpose of a warm down?

Answers 1. Increase your pulse rate by raising the blood flow to the muscles. **2.** Complete stretching exercises for the large muscle groups. **3.** Refresh a few specific skill-related practices. **4.** Prepare your mind for the activity ahead. **5.** The purpose of the warm down is to help your body to recover after exercise.

Principles of training

Principles of training

- For a physical fitness training programme to be effective you need to apply the training principles of specificity and progressive overload to your programme.
- This can be achieved by adapting duration, intensity and frequency in your programme.

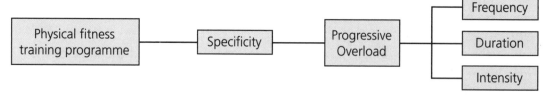

Why is specificity important?

- Specificity is the first key principle in training and is crucial for physical fitness improvement.
- Specificity involves ensuring that training is specific to your needs, relevant to the activity you are performing in and to your existing levels of fitness and ability.

Specificity	Specificity (in action)
Specific to your needs	Specific to your future fitness goals as a guard in basketball.
Specific to the activity / your role	Specific to the game of basketball, e.g. training reflects the physical demands of playing basketball games.
Specific to your fitness level	Specific to the speed and endurance (cardiorespiratory and muscular) demands of basketball.
Specific to your ability level	Specific to your performance strengths and weaknesses.

Why is progressive overload important?

- Progressive overload is the second key principle in training and is crucial to physical fitness improvement.
- You progressively add to the demands of your physical fitness programme as your training progresses. If you do not progressively overload your training, your training will cease to be useful as it will become too easy.
- For example, if you are an athlete training for the 1500 m, you could set time targets for different parts of your training programme. Once you have achieved these time targets, you could create new time targets to ensure progressive overload is included in your training.

Top Tip

The progressive overload principle can be **adapted** by varying the **frequency**, the **intensity** and the **duration** of your training.

Why is frequency important?

- Frequency determines how often you train.
- For the average performer to improve cardiorespiratory endurance, for example, you would need to exercise your heart rate within your training zone for 20 to 30 minutes for three to four sessions per week over two to three months for improvements to occur.

Why is intensity important?

- Intensity determines the relative demands of your training sessions.
- The setting of the levels of intensity is important for different aspects of physical fitness.
- Intensity can also be adapted by adjusting the **work / rest interval**.
- For a cardiorespiratory endurance programme, progressively reducing the rest intervals throughout the programme would add to the intensity of the workload (even if the actual demands of the exercises remain the same). For example,
  ▸ Week 1 / 2: 4 x 8 min run with 2 min rest @ 50% of maximum speed.
  ▸ Week 3 / 4: 4 x 8 min run with 1 min 45 sec rest @ 50% of maximum speed.
  ▸ Week 5 / 6: 4 x 8 min run with 1 min 30 sec rest @ 50% of maximum speed.
  ▸ Week 7 / 8: 4 x 8 min run with 1 min 15 sec rest @ 50% of maximum speed.

- For a muscular endurance programme, exercises would be based on a high number of repetitions with light weights. For example,

Week		Exercise	Weight lifted	Repetitions
▸ Week 1 / 3: Weight training –		Bench press	15 kg	20
▸ Week 4 / 6: Weight training –		Bench press	20 kg	20
▸ Week 7 / 9: Weight training –		Bench press	20 kg	25

- For a strength programme, exercises would be based on a low number of repetitions with heavy weights. For example,

Week		Exercise	Weight lifted	Repetitions
▸ Week 1 / 3: Weight training –		Bicep curl	15 kg	5
▸ Week 4 / 6: Weight training –		Bicep curl	18 kg	5
Week 7 / 9: Weight training –		Bicep curl	20 kg	5

Quick Test

1. Name four ways in which you can make training specific.

2. How can progressive overload principle can be adapted?

3. What does frequency determine?

4. How can intensity be adapted?

Answers 1. By making training specific to your needs, relevant to the activity you are performing in and to your existing levels of fitness and ability. 2. By varying the frequency, the intensity and the duration of your training. 3. It determines how often you train. 4. By adjusting the work / rest interval.

Principles of training

Why is duration important?

- Duration determines the length of your training time.
- Short, intensive training sessions promote anaerobic fitness improvement; longer, moderately intensive sessions develop aerobic endurance.
- Duration also applies to the length of individual sessions within a training programme (e.g. 60 minutes at the beginning rising to 80 minutes by the end of the training programme).

The dangers of over training [Credit Grade Extension]

Over training can be avoided by taking adequate rest and recovery time during training sessions. Over training can be a problem during aerobic and anaerobic training.

Aerobic training example

The task is to run around the football pitch changing between light jogging and sprinting. To avoid over training and becoming fatigued you should slow down during light jogging so that you have more time to rest and recover.

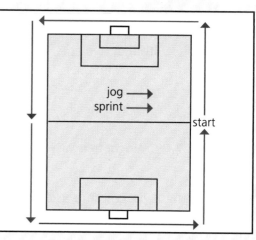

Anaerobic training example

The task is to sprint out from the goal line to line a and return, rest for 10–15 seconds, and then sprint to the edge of the penalty box (line b) and return. Rest for a further 10–15 seconds and sprint to the half way line (line c) and return. Rest for a further 10–15 seconds. Repeat this set of exercise runs a further twice.

To avoid over training you should ensure that the rest intervals are long enough for you to rest and recover. This is because it is necessary for the pulse to return to a resting level between sets to avoid over exertion.

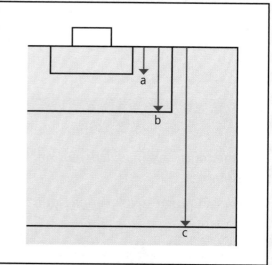

The dangers of over training

- Over training can be avoided by **adapting** the levels of frequency, intensity and duration within your training. Any of these three factors could result in over training.
- Regularly reviewing and monitoring your performance and completing a training diary, which records your thoughts about the effectiveness of your training, should be helpful in identifying which (if any) of these three factors could best be adapted to reduce the effects of over training.

Setting intensity levels for different exercises

When sprint training to improve anaerobic fitness, you need to train at a high level of intensity for short periods. During training you develop the capacity to cope with the build-up of lactic acid, which is produced by the body as a consequence of using anaerobic respiration to provide energy. After a short time, oxygen debt will lead to a high level of lactic acid build-up with the result that your muscles will tire and begin to work less effectively. For this reason lactate tolerance training programmes are completed by performers to help recovery from successive bursts of speed.

Lactate tolerance training example

During many types of activity (for example, hockey, basketball, football) players are frequently required to make short sprints without rest. Lactate tolerance drills are demanding and are deliberately designed to produce high levels of lactic acid so that the body becomes more tolerant to it and able to remove it more efficiently.

Example of a lactate tolerance drill

Task: Start at cone 1, jog to cone 4 then sprint to cone 5. Turn and jog to cone 3 and then sprint to cone 1. Turn and jog to cone 2 and sprint to cone 5. Finally, turn and sprint to cone 1. Rest for 60 seconds and repeat 2–3 times. This is one set. Complete 2–3 sets.

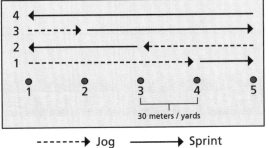

Reversibility

If you stop training then your body will revert to the condition it was in before you began training. The time this takes to occur will be dependent upon how long you trained for.

Quick Test

1. What does duration determine?

2. What is required to avoid over training?

3. What is lactate tolerance training?

Answers 1. The length of your training time. 2. Time for adequate rest and recovery. 3. Training programmes to help you recover from successive bursts of speed.

Methods / types of training

Physical fitness training methods

When organising your physical fitness training, you need to ensure that the methods of training chosen link to your specific fitness needs in a clear and obvious way. This will help ensure that your training is as beneficial as possible.

The most important methods of training for physical fitness are: continuous training, fartlek training, circuit training, weight training, flexibility and interval fitness training.

Continuous training

Definition	Types of exercises	Planned benefits
Continuous training involves training for relatively long periods where the intention is that your heart rate stays within your training zone. Exercising for 20–30 minutes for three to four times a week is one example of continuous training.		Develops cardiorespiratory endurance. Develops aerobic capacity. Easy to plan. Progressive overload can be achieved by exercising more often (increasing frequency), by exercising faster (increasing intensity) or by training for longer (increasing duration).

Fartlek training

Definition	Types of exercises	Planned benefits
Fartlek training involves continuous running or swimming with a short sprint burst followed by a slower recovery based jog or swim. Fartlek derives from the Swedish term meaning 'speed play'. Exercising for 20–30 minutes altering between top speed sprinting and slow jogging. One complete circle counts as a single repetition.	 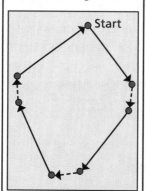	Develops aerobic and anaerobic fitness through mix of continuous running / swimming and short sprints. Can be varied to suit individual needs and can be adapted to different terrain (e.g. using short hills for speed endurance sprints during a longer aerobic run). Progressive overload achieved by exercising more often (frequency), by exercising faster (intensity) or by training for longer (increasing duration).

Circuit training (General fitness)

Definition	Types of exercises	Planned benefits
Circuit training involves general exercises which alternate the demands made on the major muscle groups as you complete the circuit.		Develops general fitness. Progressive overload achieved by increasing repetitions of circuit (frequency), decreasing rest intervals (intensity) or by training for longer (increasing duration).

Top Tip
Ensure you consider how progressive overload can be added to your chosen method of training.

Circuit training (Specific football fitness)

Definition	Types of exercises	Planned benefits
Circuit training involves specific (physical and skill-related) exercises which are beneficial for football. For example, the dribbling exercise is good for developing speed and agility, 10 press-ups and 20 sit-up exercises for upper body muscle fitness, juggling is useful for improving co-ordination and balance, and finally, hopping is good for developing agility.	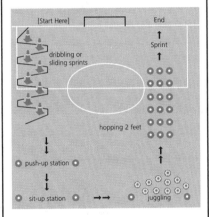	Develops specific fitness. Progressive overload achieved by increasing repetitions of circuit (frequency), decreasing rest intervals (intensity) or by training for longer (increasing duration).

Quick Test

1. Name five different methods of physical fitness training.

2. Name three advantages of continuous training.

3. Explain how progressive overload can be added for a circuit training which is based on improving general fitness.

Answers 1. Continuous training, fartlek training, circuit training, weight training and interval fitness training. **2.** Develops cardiorespiratory endurance and aerobic capacity, and is also easy to plan. **3.** Progressive overload can be achieved by increasing repetitions of circuit (frequency), decreasing rest intervals (intensity) or by training for longer (increasing duration).

Methods / types of training

Weight training

Definition	Types of exercises	Planned benefits
Weight training involves isotonic exercises in which you move the weight through the range of movement required. For example, in the squats exercise you push your legs upwards into a full standing position. Weight training also involves isometric exercises in which you hold and resist against the weight. For example, you could hold a press-up position close to the ground for a few seconds to develop your static strength.		Develops both general and specific muscles. Develops muscular endurance as well as strength and power. Straightforward to calculate personal training values (e.g. 40% to 50% of your maximum single lift if based on sets and repetitions for muscular endurance, or 80% if based on strength or power). Progressive overload achieved by increasing weight (intensity) or by increasing repetition (frequency).

Flexibility training

Definition	Types of exercises	Planned benefits
Flexibility training involves active or passive stretching or resistance exercises. For example, the standing exercise shown is useful for stretching the muscles at the front of the thigh (quadriceps). The two sitting exercises shown are useful for stretching the muscles of the lower back and the back of the thigh (hamstrings).		Increases range of movement around a joint. Progressive overload achieved by carrying out the programme more often (frequency), by working at more advanced and demanding stretching exercises (intensity) or by exercising for longer (duration).

Interval fitness training

Definition	Types of exercises	Planned benefits
Interval fitness training involves any form of exercise where the work / rest interval can be easily calculated. For example, a running training programme for a 1500m runner could use 4 x 400m repetitions completed in 60 seconds with 90 seconds recovery. This causes less fatigue than a single 1500m run.		Enables high intensity work to be undertaken with limited fatigue occurring. Progressive overload achieved by carrying out the programme more often (frequency), by working faster or decreasing rest intervals (intensity) or by exercising for longer (duration).

Top Tip

Interval fitness training can be used to develop aerobic and anaerobic capacity.

Interval fitness training

This form of training enables you to work at a high level of intensity followed by periods of rest. This helps you to train for a long time (duration) without getting too tired.

The type of running shown in the diagram is a good form of interval training. You jog for 30m then run for 40m at 50% of your fastest speed, then run for 50m at 75% of your fastest speed. After this you go back to jogging. This allows you time to recover. The distance involved as you go 'round the triangle' builds up. So as you keep running, this type of interval training becomes useful for developing cardiorespiratory endurance.

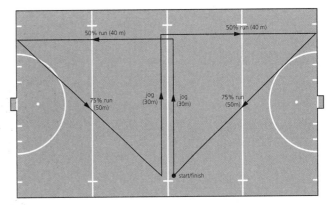

Quick Test

1. How can progressive overload be added in flexibility training?
2. What interval ratio must you calculate for interval fitness training to be effective?

Training within activities

Introduction

- To develop **physical fitness** you can either train through a **conditioning** approach (training through activity) or by completing a **fitness training** programme outside the activity (for example by completing a circuit or weight training programme).

Top Tip

Whether you train within or outside of activities, make sure you follow relevant training principles.

Advantages of fitness training within activities

You have the chance to improve physical fitness and skills and techniques at the same time.		When swimming the butterfly stroke it is useful to work on my technique and fitness at the same time.
Motivation can increase when fitness training is within activities.		I was motivated to wake up early and go swimming training.
Practice is realistic; you can still train when fatigued.		Training while playing tennis games was demanding.

Advantages of fitness training outside of activities

You can develop one specific aspect of fitness.	I prefer to complete flexibility training exercises which are specific to my needs in gymnastics.
It is easy to plan and organise.	I like to go for a run when it suits me best.
You can choose the type of training which suits your needs best.	I prefer weight training as it is easier for me to calculate my own personal training values.

[Credit Grade extension]

The diagram below is an example of a conditioning exercise. This could be used by a hockey player in order to develop her speed as well as her other hockey skills, such as dribbling.

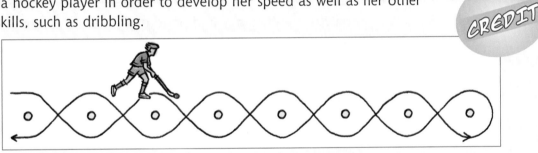

The diagram below is another example of a conditioning exercise. This exercise could be used by a basketball player to improve speed and court movement.

In this exercise you run forward from the start position under the basket to point A on the court. Next, you change direction and shuffle backwards with your hands in a defensive ready position to reach point B. Then, you side-step towards the basket, jump as high as you can and land. Repeat the exercise by moving to points C and D. Repeat for 6–8 repetitions with a 60-second rest between each repetition.

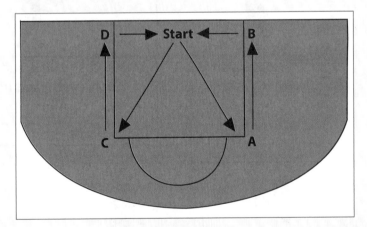

Quick Test

1. Name three advantages of training within activities.
2. Name three advantages of training outside of activities.

Skills and techniques

Introduction

- A skill describes the purpose of linked sequences of movement.
- Technique describes the ways of completing a skill.

In badminton, serving is a skill. Low and high serves are techniques for serving.

	Skill: Serving	Technique: Low serve
	Skill: Serving	Technique: High serve

Skills should be carried out with **maximum efficiency** and performed with the **minimum of effort**. This means skills and technique can be completed without becoming physically tired. A skilful performer is one who can control physical movement and can **anticipate** what is going to happen next as different skills and techniques are completed.

Study closely the pictures of the golfer who is playing a short iron (a six or seven iron) shot.

Top-Tip
Complex skills involve more decision-making than simple skills.

The open stance with feet shoulder-width apart.	Smooth backswing and turning of the shoulders and hips.	On the downswing the hands remain ahead of the club. The knees, hips and shoulders drive towards the ball.

Move forward and adopt the ready position close to the net with racquet in front of you. Watch opponent closely.	Move towards the ball with racquet, hands and upper body.	Complete short 'punch' like volley. Keeping the racquet head tilted slightly backwards (open) helps keep the ball low as it bounces in the court.	Follow through in the direction of the volley. Return to ready position as soon as possible and prepare for next shot.

Effects of skills and techniques on performance

Simple skills

- Simple (basic) skills are composed of physical actions which are common to many activities such as kicking, jumping, striking, throwing, stretching and rotating.
- You learn these basic skills (moves) as you grow. This is one reason why taking part in a varied range of physical activities is so useful for your later sporting development.
- Simple skills have basic movement patterns and require only modest decision-making.

Complex skills

- Complex skills involve difficult movements and greater decision-making than simple skills.

Simple and complex skills compared

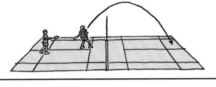

	When drawn to the net in badminton, a basic skill is to return the shuttle high to the back of the opponent's court with an underarm clear.
	A complex skill would be to try an angled drop-shot.

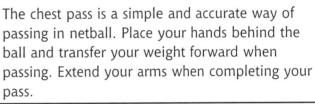	The chest pass is a simple and accurate way of passing in netball. Place your hands behind the ball and transfer your weight forward when passing. Extend your arms when completing your pass.
	This more difficult pass is used when trying to pass forward quickly in attack. You catch the ball when running and pass the ball after jumping in the air. You need to keep your head up to see you team mates and pass when in the air following a one-footed take-off.

Quick Test

1. What is the difference between a skill and a technique?

2. Why should skills be completed with maximum efficiency and performed with the minimum of effort?

3. Name two ways in which complex skills are more demanding than basic skills.

Answers 1. A skill describes the purpose of linked sequences of movement and a technique describes the ways of completing a skill. **2.** Because it means that skills and technique can be completed without becoming physically tired. **3.** Complex skills involve more difficult movements and greater decision-making than simple skills.

Skills and techniques

Preparation / action / recovery

- One effective approach for measuring your technique is through analysing your preparation, action and recovery.
- This means that you analyse the beginning, middle and finish of how well a technique is completed.
- This format is particularly useful for measuring and analysing a **single technique**.

Here are two examples. The first one outlines the criteria a goalkeeper in football could use for analysing their ability to catch a high cross.

> **Top-Tip**
> The first step in using the 'preparation / action / recovery' approach is to **establish the criteria** you wish to use for analysing your technique.

Factor		Criteria
Preparation		• Watch ball carefully • Try to maintain balanced posture
Action		• Jump from short step and single foot take-off • Get hands behind the ball and catch ball at top of jump • Keep hands quite relaxed
Recovery		• Land in balance • Get ready to react quickly after securing possession

The second example outlines the criteria a skier could use for analysing their ability to complete turns in bumpy terrain (moguls).

Factor		Criteria
Preparation		• Look ahead and plan where to begin turn • Sink down slightly, weight evenly balanced on both skis
Action		• Plant ski pole on bump top • Turn (pivot) legs and turn skis
Recovery		• Extend legs and steer skis across slope • Look ahead and prepare for next turn

Overcoming problems in skill learning

- When you practise skills it can be frustrating if you appear not to be making progress.
- The first step to making skill training effective is to identify your performance strengths and weaknesses. This will help identify any specific improvements in skills / techniques required.
- Next, you can compare your performance with a model performer. This helps highlight the specific technique weaknesses that you should focus most on improving.

Long jump example

Description of long jump				
Criteria	Fast approach run. 'Pump' with your arms and legs to increase speed.	Drive lead leg upwards. Circle your arms clockwise.	Extend legs forward.	Bend knees on landing. Reach forward with upper body.
Model performance	✔	✔	✔	✔
Your performance	✔	✗	✔	✗

Quick Test

1. What is the first step in completing analysis through a preparation / action / recovery approach?
2. What is the first step in making skill training effective?
3. What is the main benefit of comparing your performance with a model performer?

Answers 1. Establish the criteria you wish to use for analysing your technique. 2. To identify your performance strengths and weaknesses. 3. It helps highlight the specific technique weaknesses you should focus most on improving.

Skills and techniques

Skill learning environments

- High quality practice for a short time is better than long periods of repeating the same practice.
- To improve your skills and techniques you need to ensure that the 'skill learning environment' is correct for the practices you are completing.

Basketball example

The three diagrams below describe three different shooting practices in basketball. To ensure the 'skill learning environment' is correct for you would involve selecting whichever of the three practices most suited your ability. If you started with the most demanding practice (practice 3) and found it too difficult your shooting would not improve as much as you would like. It would be better to start with either practice 1 or 2 and progress as your ability improves.

Top-Tip
Skills and techniques vary in difficulty according to their requirements, your ability and your previous experience.

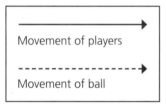

Movement of players

Movement of ball

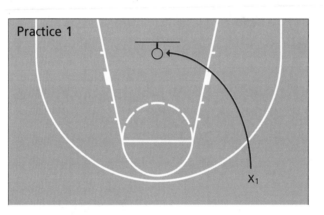

Practice 1

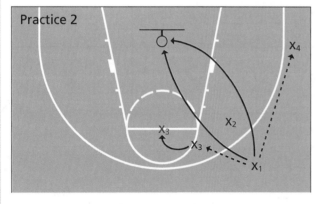

Practice 2

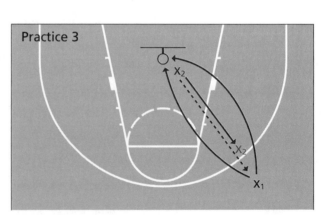

Practice 3

Skills and techniques – [Credit Grade Extension]

Skill is **relative** to ability. For example, your ability to complete different balances and movements on the beam in gymnastics will be determined by your level of ability. Analyse the five pictures and identify the balances and movements which are most complex to complete.

Skill learning also requires consideration of the degree of **decision-making** involved in completing skills and technique.

The 100m sprinter requires the ability to repeat straightforward repetitions or sets of movements. However, sprinting only requires a relatively low level of decision-making.

By contrast, the rugby player has more decisions to make as he attempts to protect the ball as well as 'hand-off' the defender who is trying to tackle him. In addition, the attacker has to have **awareness** of where other players are in his team and make decisions about whether attempting to pass or retain possession is the better option.

Top-Tip
Complex skills require more information processing than simple basic skills as they are more intricate. For this reason they require more time to learn and more specific training to develop.

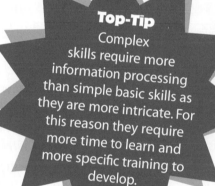

Quick Test

1. When selecting a skill or technique practice what variables should you consider?

Answers 1. You should consider the requirements of the skill or technique, your level of ability and your previous experience of the skill or technique.

Skills learning

Safe practice

When learning skills you need to ensure practice is safe. This means you should make sure that practice is at the right level for your ability, and complete a warm up before practice and a warm down after practice. You also need to understand and abide by the safety rules for specific activities.

Trampoline example

In trampoline, safe practice relates to both your role as a performer and as a supporter. As a performer you need to get on and off the trampoline carefully and, when bouncing, attempt to remain over the middle of the trampoline. You need to try to bounce in a controlled way with as little sideways, forwards and backwards movement as possible.

You also need to follow more general safety issues. These include ensuring that the trampoline and working area are safely set out. It also involves ensuring that nobody in the class moves underneath the trampoline when another classmate is bouncing on it.

Top-Tip
Learning skills involves: considering safe practice, methods of practice and how best to practise with a partner and in a group.

In addition, you need to follow precise teacher instructions and advice about when more demanding movements like somersaults can be attempted. For somersaults, a feature of safe practice often involves students (or teachers and students) working co-operatively. During co-operative practice it is important that you try to understand both performer and supporter roles so that practice is safe.

Practice methods

Three main practice methods are: gradual build-up, whole / part / whole and passive / active practices.

Gradual build-up

Gradual build-up is the learning of a skill in stages with each stage becoming increasingly difficult. It is a useful practice method for learning complex (difficult) skills. It is useful for practising at a level which is appropriate to your ability. You can then progress to the next practice when ready. This allows you to develop confidence in your ability.

An example of this is learning a flight dive in swimming.

Top-Tip
Practice should be challenging but achievable.

Quick Test

1. Name three practice methods.

2. How can confidence develop through gradual build-up practice?

Skills learning

Gradual build-up

A second example of the gradual build-up practice method is practising your forehand shots with the intention of hitting shots with ever greater accuracy and depth.

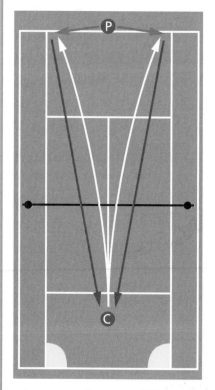

C Coach P Player ☐ Target

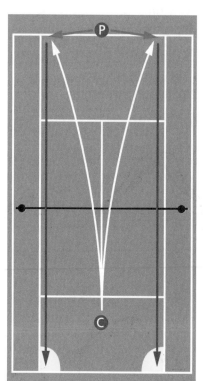

C Coach P Player ☐ Target

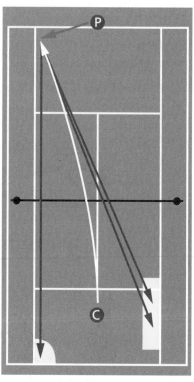

C Coach P Player ☐ Target

Explanation

Stage 1: The performer plays a forehand return to the feeder. The performer adjusts footwork as necessary, turn body sideways on and plays a forehand return.

Stage 2: The performer plays a forehand down the line in order to move imaginary opponent away from the centre of the court. The performer moves in dynamic balance from the centre of the back of the court to their right hand side and adjusts their footwork and body shape to play the return shot.

Stage 3: The performer plays either a forehand down the line or a cross-court attacking shot. The performer has to move and decide which shot to play.

Similar practices to these could be completed for backhand return shots.

Whole / part / whole

Whole / part / whole is often used as a practice method by performers who already have some experience of the activity. This is because this practice method works best when you can perform the whole skill already. After analysing your strengths and weaknesses you can work on improving the problem part then practice the whole skill again. Once this is completed the whole skill or technique can be performed again.

Top-Tip
Skills which can easily be separated into parts suit the whole / part / whole practice method best.

High jump example

In the high jump, if your initial jumps showed that your run up and approach were weak, then you could practise this part of the jumping technique on its own until it improved. This would involve focusing on the speed and arc of your run and ensuring that you were able to take off from exactly the spot intended. Once this had improved you could practise the whole jumping action again.

Trampoline example

If, during your whole 15-bounce trampoline sequence, there was a technique problem during the middle part of the sequence, whole / part / whole practice could be useful. Practice would focus on practising the particular bounces in the middle of the sequence where improvement was required. For example, if bounce 8 (a front somersault) was a performance weakness you would start with bounces 5 to 7 to get into the sequence and then practise the somersault, complete the next bounce (bounce 9) and stop. Once this short sequence of five bounces had improved you could practise the whole sequence again.

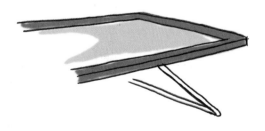

Quick Test

1. What types of skills and technique benefit most from whole / part / whole practice?

Skills learning

Passive / active practices

It is often useful to practise with partners as they can vary the degree of opposition required to help you improve.

Football example

In this practice the two attacking players in the middle of the centre circle try to retain possession of the ball. The attacking players can pass the ball to the four players on the outside of the circle and receive a return pass from them, or the players on the outside of the circle can pass to the other attacking player.

At the beginning the defenders try to provide passive opposition by only moving relatively slowly when attempting to gain possession of the ball. As the ability of the attacking players improves the defenders can provide active opposition by moving more quickly when trying to gain possession of the ball.

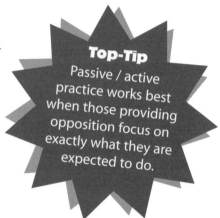

Top-Tip
Passive / active practice works best when those providing opposition focus on exactly what they are expected to do.

Stages of learning [Credit Grade Extension]

There are **three important stages** in learning and developing skills: these are often referred to as the planning stage, the practice stage and the automatic stage. For credit grade you need to understand in detail the automatic stage of skill learning. Information on the other stages is provided in order to indicate how progression to the automatic stage of skill learning occurs.

The planning stage

During the planning stage, you find out what the skill involves. You establish what the parts of the skill are and make your first attempt at learning each part. Errors are likely to be common at this stage, so you need advice, encouragement and support to make progress.

Planning stage – Badminton high serve (singles) example
<ul><li>You get used to the grip of the racquet.</li><li>You get used to standing sideways on, swinging the racquet and hitting the shuttlecock.</li><li>You gradually get used to transferring your weight forward when swinging the racquet.</li><li>You make quite a lot of errors – the swing and hitting action lack control and fluency. (This might mean you miss hitting the shuttlecock altogether at times.)</li><li>The shuttlecock often travels in different directions.</li><li>You take advice from teachers / friends.</li></ul> 

At this stage of skill learning if 10 practice serves were attempted this is where the serves might well land. Note how the serves cover a wide area at this stage of skill learning. Only one serve has landed in the ideal target area at the back of the court and four serves landed outside the service reception area.

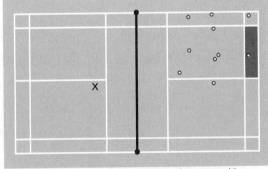

X = service start position   O = service start position
■ = ideal target area

Quick Test

1. Name the **three stages** of skill learning.

2. Why do you need advice, encouragement and support at the planning stage of skill learning?

Skills learning

Stages of learning [Credit Grade Extension]

The practice stage

During the practice stage you link together all the required parts of the skill.

Practice stage – Badminton high serve (singles) example
<ul><li>The service action is becoming more fluent as the hitting action links to transferring weight forward.</li><li>There are fewer errors – the swing and hitting actions are more controlled, and serves are becoming more accurate, although some further refinement is still necessary.</li><li>You become less reliant on teacher advice and are able to evaluate your own performance in general.</li></ul>	

At this stage of skill learning if 10 practice serves were attempted this is where the serves might well land. Note how the serves cover a narrower area than at the planning stage of skill learning. Three serves have landed in the ideal target area at the back of the court and three serves have landed outside the service reception area.

X = service start position   O = service start position
= ideal target area

Top-Tip
During the practice stage, quality practice will help reduce the number of mistakes made during performance.

The automatic stage

At this stage, errors are less likely and most key parts of a skill have become automatic. As a result, little attention is paid to them.

Automatic stage – Badminton high serve (singles) example

• The service action is becoming fluent and precise as the hitting action is smooth and consistent.

• There are very few errors or inconsistencies in the service action.

• As most of the service action has become automatic you now have the chance to pay selective attention to other aspects of the service action. For example, you can observe closely where your opponent is standing and vary where exactly within the service reception area you aim towards.

• You become less reliant on teacher advice and are able to evaluate which specific aspects of your service action require improvement.

At this stage of skill learning if 10 practice serves were attempted this is where the serves might well land. Note how the serves cover a narrower area than at the practice stage of skill learning. Six serves have landed in the ideal target area at the back of the court and only one serve landed out of the service reception area.

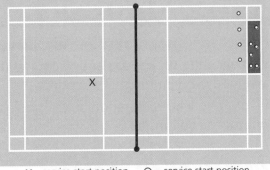

X = service start position   O = service start position
■ = ideal target area

Quick Test

1. Why do you become less reliant on teacher advice during the practice stage?

2. Why is it advantageous for most key parts of a skill have become automatic?

Answers 1. Because you are able to evaluate your own performance in general. **2.** Because it allows you to pay selective attention to other key aspects of performance.

Principles of effective practice and refinement

Top-Tip
Working out the work to rest ratio is one of the key issues in making skill practice specific to your needs.

Introduction

In general for practice to be effective

- practice should have clear and achievable objectives
- practice must be specific to improving your skill and technique weaknesses
- practice should avoid becoming too repetitive as this will affect your level of motivation as well as lead to you becoming tired and fatigued
- practice should be interesting and enjoyable
- practice should be based on your existing level of ability.

Compare the two kayakers. They are both practising techniques which suit their ability.

A kayaker paddling on flat water

A kayaker paddling in rapid water

The benefits of variation in practice

- Having varied practices is one effective way of **reducing boredom**.
- In swimming, for example, varying the strokes you are swimming can make practice more enjoyable and motivate you to keep practising.
- Training for too long a time can also lead to boredom and a gradual reduction in the amount of progress you make.

How long to practise

- Another principle of effective practice is that you practise for a suitable **training time**.
- Too short and improvements will be limited. Too long and you may become fatigued and prone to suffering an injury.
- The correct training time will depend upon the demands of the activity. For some activities, such as swimming, and for longer distance running events in athletics, training times are usually long. For other activities, such as throwing and sprinting events in athletics, training times tend to be shorter.

Training times will also depend on your **level of ability**. When you are a beginner you tend to practise for less time than if you are a more able performer. If you are practising long distance running events your training time will increase as your ability increases.

Work-to-rest ratio

When practising you need to calculate the ratio of work relative to rest. The work-to-rest ratio is based on

- your previous experience in the activity
- your level of practical ability
- the difficulties of the skills and techniques involved
- the physical demands involved in the practice.

Basketball: Full court layup shooting practice

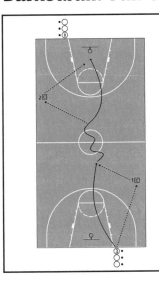

Player 3 passes to feeder 1. Feeder 1 passes the ball back to player 3.

Player 3 then passes to feeder 2 and cuts towards the basket and receives a pass from feeder 2 and completes a layup shot.

After player 3 finishes the layup shot, player 4 passes to feeder 2 and feeder 1 for a layup shot at opposite end of the court, and so the practice continues.

When players receive the first pass they can dribble once before passing to the next feeder.

The work to rest ratio in this practice is one part work and five parts rest and recovery. This is a good ratio to have as the practice is active and demanding and completed at a quick speed.

Practising under pressure [Credit]

With skills and technique that you can complete with a high degree of control and fluency it is important to practise when under pressure. This will make practice realistic and similar to when you perform in competition. In team activities this could involve increasing the demands of opponents during practice. Practising under pressure can also involve individual activities such as swimming. For example, when completing sets of 100m front crawl time swims, you could often practise with another swimmer beside you. This makes practice more realistic.

Quick Test

1. Name five general features of effective practice.
2. The work-to-rest ratio is based on four factors. Name them.

Answers 1. **Practice should have clear and achievable objectives**; it should be specific to improving your skill and technique weaknesses; it should avoid becoming too repetitive as this will affect your level of motivation as well as lead to you becoming tired and fatigued; it should be interesting and enjoyable; it should be based on your existing level of ability. 2. Your previous experience in the activity; your level of practical ability; the difficulties of the skills and techniques involved; the physical demands involved in the practice.

Feedback and co-operation

Introduction

Feedback is information you receive about your performance. Positive feedback helps your performance improve. For feedback to be effective it needs to be precise, accurate and be provided as soon as possible after an activity. Feedback involves analysis about the decisions you make before and during an activity.

INPUT
Judge whether to play low or high serve, watching where opponents are standing.

DECISION-MAKING
Decide to play high serve.

INPUT
Complete high serve.

FEEDBACK
Assess results – was playing a high serve a good idea? Did it land at the back of the court as intended?

INPUT
Judge quality of set pass and position of blockers.

DECISION-MAKING
Decide to play attacking 'spike' shot.

INPUT
Complete spike shot.

FEEDBACK
Assess results – was playing a spike a good idea? Did I hit the spike to the correct part of opponent's court?

INPUT
Judge the speed you are running at relative to the distance which you have to run to complete course.

DECISION-MAKING
Decide whether to increase speed, keep speed the same or slow down a little to conserve energy.

INPUT
Continue running.

FEEDBACK
Assess results – was decision to increase speed, keep speed the same or slow down a little to conserve energy correct?

INPUT
Assess where opponent is and the speed and spin of the ball.

DECISION-MAKING
Decide to play forehand down the line shot instead of hitting across court.

INPUT
Complete forehand shot.

FEEDBACK
Assess results – was a forehand down the line shot the best shot to play?

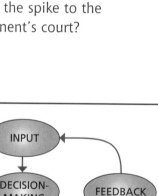

Collecting information about performance

You can receive feedback by evaluating advice you receive from teachers and class mates. When offering feedback, try to focus on the most important points necessary for improvement and identify specific strengths and weaknesses. Comparing observed performance against criteria on checklists is one popular method for providing feedback.

The example below shows the results of a small-sided hockey game lasting 30 minutes each half. The information contains details about the effectiveness of passing in different directions when under different levels of pressure and at different times.

Game Analysis Sheet

Team: Scotstown Academy **Role:** Attacker

Opposition: Central High School **Date:** 25/11/06

✔ = effective ✘ = ineffective

Time (minutes	Pass forward under pressure	Pass forward under less pressure	Pass to side or back under pressure	Pass to side or back under little pressure
1st half 0–10	✔✔✘✘✘	✔	✔	✔✔
0–19	✔✘✘	✔✔	✔✔	✔
21–30	✘✘	✘✔	✘✘	✘
2nd half 0–10	✔		✔	✔✔✔
11–19	✔✘✘	✔✔	✔	✔✘
21–30	✘✔✘	✔✘	✔✘✘	✔

Task: From the results in the diagram what feedback would you offer the performer? Specifically, what happens to their level of effectiveness at passing in the last part of the first half and last part of the second half?

Quick Test

1. What is needed for feedback to be effective?

2. Name one popular method for providing feedback.

Answers **1.** Feedback needs to be precise, accurate and provided as soon as possible after activity. **2.** Comparing observed performance against criteria on checklists.

Feedback and co-operation

Knowledge of results

Comparing knowledge of results is another popular method for providing feedback. The example below shows the types of points scoring which led to the final result in a rugby union game.

Team A	**22**		
Team B	**13**		

Points scored		**Scoring: Tries**	
First half	14 6	Total	3 1
Second half	8 7	First half 2 0 Second half 1 1	

Scoring			
Conversions made	2 1	Conversions missed	1 0
Penalty goals scored	1 2	Penalty goals missed	2 2

Knowledge of results information can go beyond mentioning the outcomes of a game or performance. Continuing with the rugby example mentioned above, knowledge of results is also useful for describing how different skills and techniques within the game were performed. This example uses games statistics to describe performance.

Team A		Team B
75	Passes completed	66
60	Tackles made	54
16	Tackles missed	23
8	Scrums won on put in	7
1	Scrums lost on put in	4
12	Lineouts won on throw	9
1	Lineouts lost on throw	4
12	Turnovers won	9

Top-Tip
Accepting responsibility is a key part of working co-operatively as part of a team / group.

Kinaeshetic awareness

As well as being provided with feedback about your performance you can evaluate your performance through the **internal** feedback you receive. This is easier to do as your performance level improves. Internal feedback is often referred to as 'kinaesthetic awareness' and refers to the 'feel' of different sporting actions. For example, in golf, as your ability improves, you are likely to be able to 'feel' whether or not your shot is accurate as you complete your golf swing.

Co-operation

In the different activities in your Standard Grade course it is important that you can effectively co-operate with class mates. This involves **co-operating when performing**. The setter in volleyball has to co-operate with the player spiking the ball. This involves practising together and talking about how best the set and spike can be completed.

Co-operation also involves observing a partner and **recording information**. This involves being a critical friend to your partner and team mates. You watch and note down information carefully and offer feedback on specific skills and general encouragement. You develop trust with your partner.

When participating as part of a team working co-operatively involves **accepting responsibility** and recognising your role within a team. In a zone defence in basketball it is important that you co-operate with others to keep the correct shape for your team as a unit.

Accepting responsibility also involves helping your partner. In trampoline, for example, providing safety and support can help your partner.

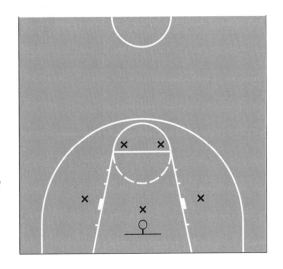

Quick Test

1. What is another name for internal feedback?

2. Name three common ways in which effective co-operation can occur?

Answers **1.** Kinaesthetic awareness. **2.** It can occur through co-operating when performing with partner, group or team, or by co-operating when recording information, or by co-operating through accepting responsibility.

Balance

Introduction

- Balance is the ability to retain the centre of gravity over your base of support.
- Balancing requires the control of different groups of muscles.
- A lower centre of gravity provides stability when balancing.

Top-Tip
The larger the base of support the easier it is to remain in balance. The smaller the base of support the more difficult it is to remain in balance.

Gymnastics, hockey and athletics examples

Type of balance		Skill / technique: How balance is achieved and maintained
Static balances such as a headstand in gymnastics require you to hold a balance.		The movements into and out of the balance are slow and controlled. The major muscles involved in the balance have good body tension. In the headstand this involves the stomach and leg muscles. This benefits posture as the hips remain above the shoulders. The large triangular base of support created by the placement of forehead and hands provides stability during the balance.

Type of balance		Skill / technique: How balance is achieved and maintained
Dynamic balances such as dribbling in hockey require you to maintain balance while running and frequently changing direction and body shape.		By flexing and adjusting your body shape it is possible to keep your centre of gravity over your base of support. Good body tension helps when running and changing direction.

Type of balance		Skill / technique: How balance is achieved and maintained
The sprint start position is a static balance. When sprinting begins it is a dynamic balance.		When completing a sprint start in athletics the centre of gravity is over the base of support. Most of the weight is on your arms. This enables you to drive off your leading (front) foot when you hear the start signal.

Balance

The greater **stability** provided by a low centre of gravity and large base of support make it easier to control the movements into and out of a balance. For example, when learning the headstand you can move to a tucked headstand position first. When you are in control of your movements to this point you can slowly use the benefits of your stable base of support and low centre of gravity to extend and straighten your legs. By contrast the higher centre of gravity and the smaller base of support make the handstand a more demanding technique.

In dynamic balances you need to adjust your body position to remain in balance. For example, in a single continuous action such as a golf swing you need to ensure at the start of the swing that you are well balanced. This usually involves ensuring that your feet are close to shoulder-width apart.

In an ongoing continuous action, such as hurdling in athletics, you need to ensure that by adjusting your body shape your hurdle position is similar at each hurdle. This will involve an alternate leg / arm action. For example, if you lead with your left leg you need to ensure your upper body and right arm are leaning forward. The position of your right arm helps ensure that you remain in dynamic balance.

Quick Test

Complete the missing words

1. Balance is the ability to retain the centre of gravity over your ---- of support.

2. Balancing requires the control of different groups of -------.

3. A lower centre of gravity provides -------- when balancing.

4. Some balances are static, others balances are called ------- balances.

Answers 1. base. 2. muscles. 3. stability. 4. dynamic.

Transfer of weight and application of force

Transfer of weight

- For a whole variety of different skills and techniques you need to transfer your weight for effective performance.
- At times, this can be in single actions such as throwing the javelin. At other times, for example when running, simple actions are repeated.

Top-Tip
Transfer of weight can help increase power in striking, throwing or kicking actions.

Activity	Skill / technique	Type of action		Transfer of weight	Benefit
Softball	Hitting	Striking		As you watch the pitch you begin to bring the bat down and transfer your weight forward.	Transferring your weight forward allows you to achieve a powerful strike as the muscles of your legs and upper body are used.
Rugby union	Drop kick	Kicking		As you drop the ball onto the ground you kick the ball. You transfer your weight forward by bringing your kicking foot through when striking the ball.	Transferring your weight forward allows you to get the right height and distance on the drop kick.
Athletics	Javelin	Throwing		At the beginning of the throw the weight is on the rear foot. As you complete the throw you transfer your weight forward from your back foot to your front foot.	Transferring your weight forward allows you to achieve a powerful throw as the muscles of your legs, upper body are used.

For some skills and techniques the transfer of weight can be from legs to arms and back to legs. A handspring in gymnastics is an example of this type of transference of weight.

Application of force

- When performing different skills and techniques different forces are applied and resisted.
- For every action there is an equal and opposite reaction (Newton's Third Law).
- The more powerful muscles contractions are, the greater the force which can be applied.

Activity	Skill / technique	Type of action		Application of force	Benefit
Swimming	Backstroke	Starting		As I push backwards against the wall, I am powerfully extending and straightening my legs.	This enables me to get into my swimming stroke quickly after my push off and glide are complete.
Basketball	Rebounding	Jumping		As I push down against the floor, I am powerfully extending and straightening my legs.	This enables me to jump high and secure possession of the ball.

Application of force [Credit Grade Extension]

If speed is required then the greater the force applied the better. Differences in the mass of the body will affect performance. If the force applied to the sprinting block is the same, the athlete with the smaller mass will accelerate at a quicker rate.

Quick Test

1. Name three types of action where transfer of weight might help skilful performance.
2. Name a skill or technique where transfer of weight is from legs to arms and back to legs.

Answers 1. Striking, throwing or kicking actions. 2. Handspring, Cartwheel.

Rotation and resistance

- Rotation is the movement of the body (or part of the body) around a central axis. In different activities you rotate (turn) in order to carry out effective skills and techniques.

Discus example

Top-Tip
When you apply force there will be resistance.

When throwing the discus in athletics you turn around in a spinning back-to-front movement to generate power. This is a complex technique. You build up speed before throwing by quickly turning your feet around. After the throw you follow through and keep turning until you have regained your balance.

Trampoline example

As well as rotating around you also can rotate by turning head over heels. The tighter the tuck the quicker you will rotate. Rotation is important when completing a front somersault in trampolining.

Gymnastics example

Another form of rotation is when you turn sideways. A cartwheel – where you turn over from feet to hand, balancing on the ground before returning to feet on the ground – is an example of this type of rotation.

Resistance

Resistance can either be an advantage or a disadvantage. When sprinting in athletics the starting blocks are an advantage. They provide a resistance. By powerfully straightening the legs against the starting blocks the sprinter can  quickly gain speed. The track creates a helpful resistance as you continue running. If you are running into a headwind this would be unhelpful.

Force overcoming resistance is important in swimming. Consider the diagram below.

First swimmer   *Second swimmer*

In this example, the first swimmer is having difficulty in swimming effectively due to the resistance created by poor streamlining. This is evident through the swimmer's lower centre of gravity. With the second swimmer the leg action is more effective, less water is displaced, the swimmer's centre of gravity is higher. Overall, the forces applied are overcoming the resistance created by the water in a more effective way.

Quick Test

1. Describe three different types of rotation.

2. Explain why effective streamlining is an advantage in swimming.

Answers 1. You can rotate by turning (spinning around), by turning (head over heels) or by turning sideways (feet to hand to feet). **2.** Effective streamlining means that you will create less resistance. This means your centre of gravity will be higher and you will displace less water.

Follow through

When completing different skills and techniques it is important for effective performance that kicking, striking / hitting and throwing actions have a good follow through. An effective follow through follows on from the preparation and action phases in different skills and techniques.

Kicking, striking / hitting and throwing examples

Top-Tip
In these examples the follow through is in the direction of the shot.

In other actions the follow through involves body rotation. The ball and socket joint in the hips and shoulder help rotation in the three different striking actions below.

Top-Tip
An effective follow through helps the accuracy and if necessary the power associated with a kicking, striking / hitting or throwing action.

Quick Test

1. Why does an effective follow through help accuracy?

Answers 1. Because it completes the action, either by following through in the direction of the kick, throw or striking action, or by using rotation as part of the follow through action.

Knowledge and Understanding and Evaluating

Knowledge and Understanding

Your course will involve you studying three areas within Knowledge and Understanding. These are: Activities; The Body; and Skills and Techniques.

Knowledge and Understanding		
Activities	**The Body**	**Skills and Techniques**
Nature and purpose	Structure and function	Techniques
Official / formal and unwritten rules	Aspects of fitness	Ways of developing skill
Roles and function	Training and its effects	Mechanical principles

Improving your Knowledge and Understanding

To improve your Knowledge and Understanding you can:

- Link information about areas of Knowledge and Understanding ('Activities', 'The Body', and 'Skills and Techniques') to the activities in your course.
- Participate in a wide variety of roles in your course – performer, official, analysing your partner practising a skill, recording information.

Examinations: Evaluating

Your course will involve you evaluating performance by observing and describing sporting actions in different activities and suggesting improvements. This will involve you in recognising basic actions, observing fitness levels and studying in detail different techniques and how they affect the development of quality performance.

Improving your Evaluating

To help improve your Evaluating abilities you can:

- Observe in detail, train your eyes to take in information and make suggestions for improvement.
- Observe and describe and suggest improvements in different activities to broaden your analytical abilities.
- Regularly review performance against different criteria.

Course assessment

The three course areas (Performance, Knowledge and Understanding and Evaluating) are assessed in different ways.

Performance

Your Performance abilities will be assessed in a minimum of four different activities **during** your course.

Foundation	Credit
Basic skills	Complex skills
High serve	Low and flick serves
Overhead clear	Overhead drop shot
Underarm clear	Backhand smash
	Overhead smash

Knowledge and Understanding

Your Knowledge and Understanding (KU) is assessed as part of an examination **at the end** of your course.

Foundation	Credit
Limited KU facts and principles.	Detailed KU and the ability to interpret facts and principles.
Can describe some limited facts and principles.	Can interpret KU gained during active learning.

Evaluating

Your evaluating ability is assessed as part of an examination **at the end** of your course.

Foundation	Credit
Identify and describe in **basic** terms different actions and make some suggestions to improve performance.	Identify and describe **in detail** different actions and make some **detailed** suggestions to improve performance.
Can make some basic performance comparisons.	Identifies specific skills needed in activities, and can describe their importance in detail.

Knowledge and Understanding and Evaluating

Knowledge and Understanding and Evaluating examination

Based on your progress during your course you will either complete the Knowledge and Understanding and Evaluating examination at Foundation and General level **or** General and Credit level. The examination lasts approximately 1 hour at both levels.

The examination question paper is in two parts: Section 1 is on Evaluating and Section 2 is on Knowledge and Understanding. All questions are in two parts and you answer both parts of each question. For the video-based evaluating questions a commentary provides instructions about how and when to answer questions.

Course weighting

Performance counts for 50% of your final mark, with Knowledge and Understanding (25%) and Evaluating (25%) making up the other 50% of your final mark. When you have completed all parts of your assessment successfully you will receive either an overall Foundation, General or Credit level award.

Index

Index

Notes